DATA-RESPON
EXERCISES
GCSE BUSIN
STUDIES

A. J. Grabham, *B.Sc.(Econ.)*
C. E. Smith, *B.Sc., M.Sc.(Econ.)*

STANLEY THORNES (PUBLISHERS) LTD

First published in 1989 by:
Stanley Thornes (Publishers) Ltd
Old Station Drive
Leckhampton
CHELTENHAM GL53 0DN
England

British Library Cataloguing in Publication Data

Grabham, A. J. (Alison J)
Data-response exercises for GCSE business studies.
1. Business enterprise
I. Title II. Smith, C. E. (Charles E)

ISBN 0-7487-0162-1

Typeset by Tech-Set, Gateshead, Tyne & Wear
Printed and bound in Great Britain at The Bath Press, Avon

CONTENTS

The section headings correspond to the five 'areas of study' listed in the National Criteria for GCSE Business Studies. However, it should be noted that many exercises contain tasks which cut across two or more of the sections.

Section I External Environment of the Business

Section II Business Structure and Organisation

Section III Business Behaviour

(A) FINANCE AND MARKETS

(B) DISTRIBUTION

Section IV People in Business

Section V Aiding and Controlling Business Activity

For Joanne Davies and Joleon Caparros

PREFACE

Data-response exercises have become increasingly used in teaching and assessment. This is especially true of GCSE Business Studies, where all the examining boards use questions of this type.

The advantages are numerous: learning is made more interesting; classroom topics are linked to relevant events in the world outside; and students are given access to a much wider range of written and graphical material than would otherwise be available. However, there are some problems, including the fact that teachers find that they quickly exhaust the material available for classwork and examination practice. It is hoped that this book will complement existing texts and add to the teacher's armoury of resources.

This is a selection of exercises which have been successfully used by actual teachers with real students. An attempt has been made to base the questions on a variety of stimulus material, so that students find them both interesting and informative. Bearing in mind the needs of mixed ability classes, the tasks range from the simple to the challenging.

Suggested answers and comments for selected questions are grouped together at the end of this book. The suggested answers and comments are 'selected' because many questions are comparatively easy and the authors feel that it would be impertinent to teach their colleagues to 'suck eggs'. Additionally, it is hoped that students will be encouraged to appreciate that many questions in Business Studies are open to a variety of responses, and no single answer should always be regarded as 'gospel'. The authors would be pleased to receive feedback from teachers using these exercises which might usefully be incorporated in the answers and comments section of future editions.

The authors

Alison Grabham and Charles Smith are experienced teachers and examiners. They both teach Business Studies and related subjects at Brynteg Comprehensive School, Bridgend, Mid Glamorgan.

Note

For their help in writing Exercises 31, 46 and 54, we are grateful to Ivor Hicks, Bryntirion Comprehensive School, Bridgend, and Alun Jones, Bridgend College of Technology. We also owe thanks to Ann Jones, Saint Martin's Comprehensive School, Caerphilly, for her support, and Mike Rigby of Stanley Thornes, whose advice has been invaluable. All errors and omissions are our own responsibility. We cannot imagine how authors would manage to write books without the full support of their families. We especially wish to thank Steven Grabham and Julia, Sally, and Matthew Smith, for their patience and tolerance.

A.J.G.
C.E.S.

ACKNOWLEDGEMENTS

Every effort has been made to contact copyright holders for permission to use material in this book. It is hoped that none have been missed, but the publishers would be grateful to hear from anyone who might not yet have given permission for material to be reproduced or adapted.

The following copyright holders are acknowledged with thanks:

Chase Manhattan Bank, Lloyds Bank, The Post Office, British Petroleum PLC, Broadcasters' Audience Research Board Ltd., The Mail Order Protection Scheme, The Advertising Standards Authority, H.M. Stationery Office (Government Statistics, including Economic Trends, Social Trends and Regional Trends), H.M. Treasury (Economic Progress Report), Times Books (*The Times 1000*), Euromonitor Publications (*The A–Z of UK Retailing, The A–Z of UK Brand Leaders*), Kompass Publishers (*UK Trade Names*), *Labour Research*, *Bridgend Recorder*, *Daily Mirror*, *The Guardian*, *The Independent*, *The Observer*, *South Wales Echo*, *Sunday Telegraph*, *The Sunday Times*, *Western Mail*, Paul Brown, Sue Stoessl.

STAGES OF PRODUCTION ·1·

EXERCISE 1

Consider these two items.

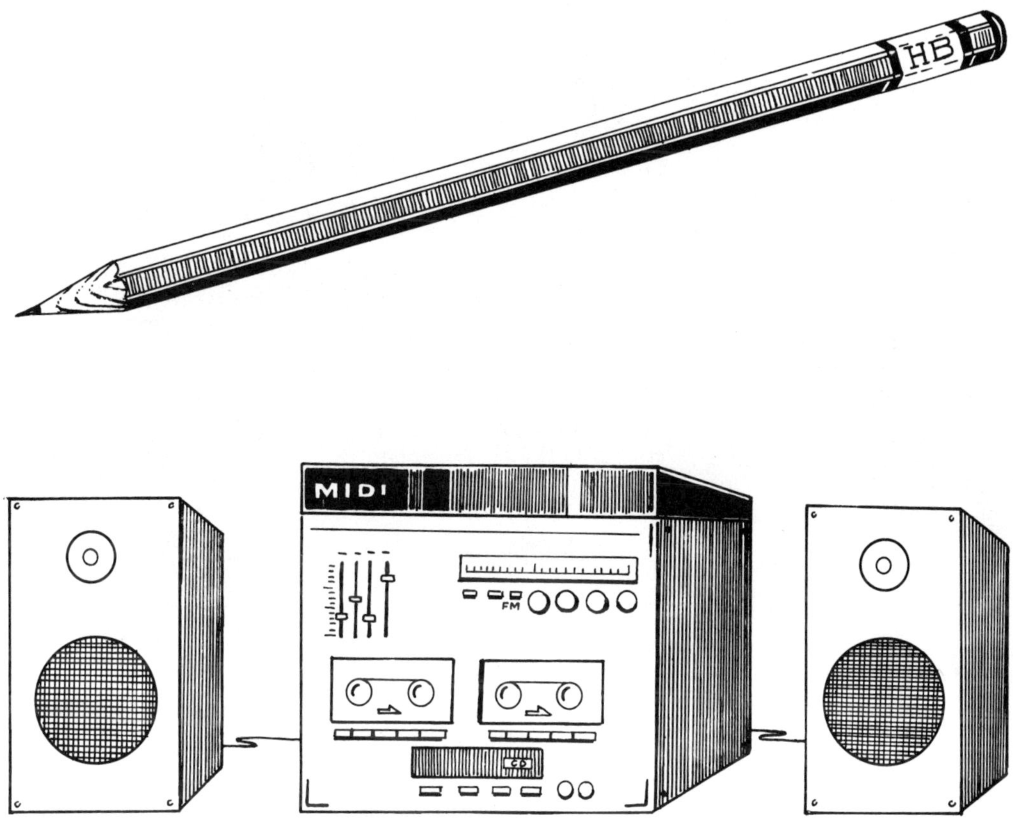

a Make as complete a list as you can of the raw materials which make up these two items.

b Trace these raw materials back to their country of origin.

c Draw a chart to illustrate your findings.

d For each of these items

i) Explain how the four factors of production (land, labour, capital and enterprise) have been used in making them.
ii) Write a paragraph to describe the three stages of their production (primary, secondary and tertiary).

STAGES OF PRODUCTION ·2·

EXERCISE 2

Study these occupations then answer the questions.

a Draw three columns headed 'Primary', 'Secondary' and 'Tertiary'. Place each of the illustrated occupations in the correct column.

b i) Make a list of the occupations of TEN adults who are known to you (members of your family, or neighbours). Decide how many of the ten belong to the primary, secondary and tertiary sectors.

ii) With the help of your teacher, combine your totals with those of other members of your class (thus, in a class of 25 you would classify the occupations of 250 people).

iii) Calculate the percentages of the class total working in the primary, secondary and tertiary sectors. Display your result as a bar diagram or pie chart. Comment on your findings.

iv) In what ways, if any, might the result of this survey have been different
1 50 years ago
2 150 years ago?

v) Which sector is likely to grow most rapidly in the near future? Give reasons for your answer. Why is this trend important for young people nearing school leaving age?

AGRICULTURE

Study these illustrations.

Labour productivity

SOURCE: WESTERN MAIL, 23 JUNE 1988

Employment generated by agriculture in the UK

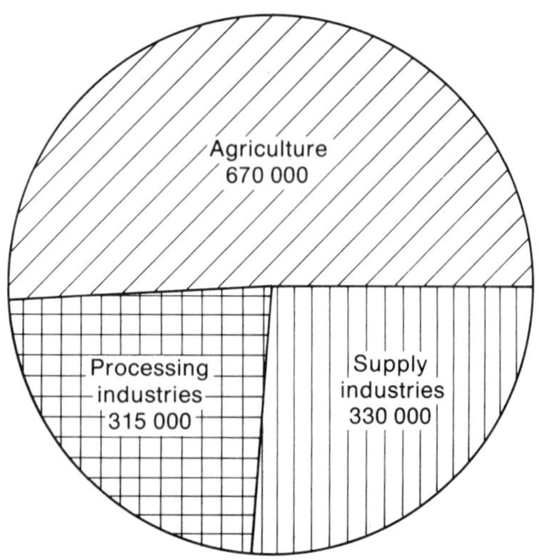

a Suggest reasons why productivity has increased at a faster rate in agriculture than in other industries.

b Explain why agriculture is important to other sectors of the economy.

THE PRICE OF UK COAL

EXERCISE 4

Study the following graph carefully and then answer the questions.

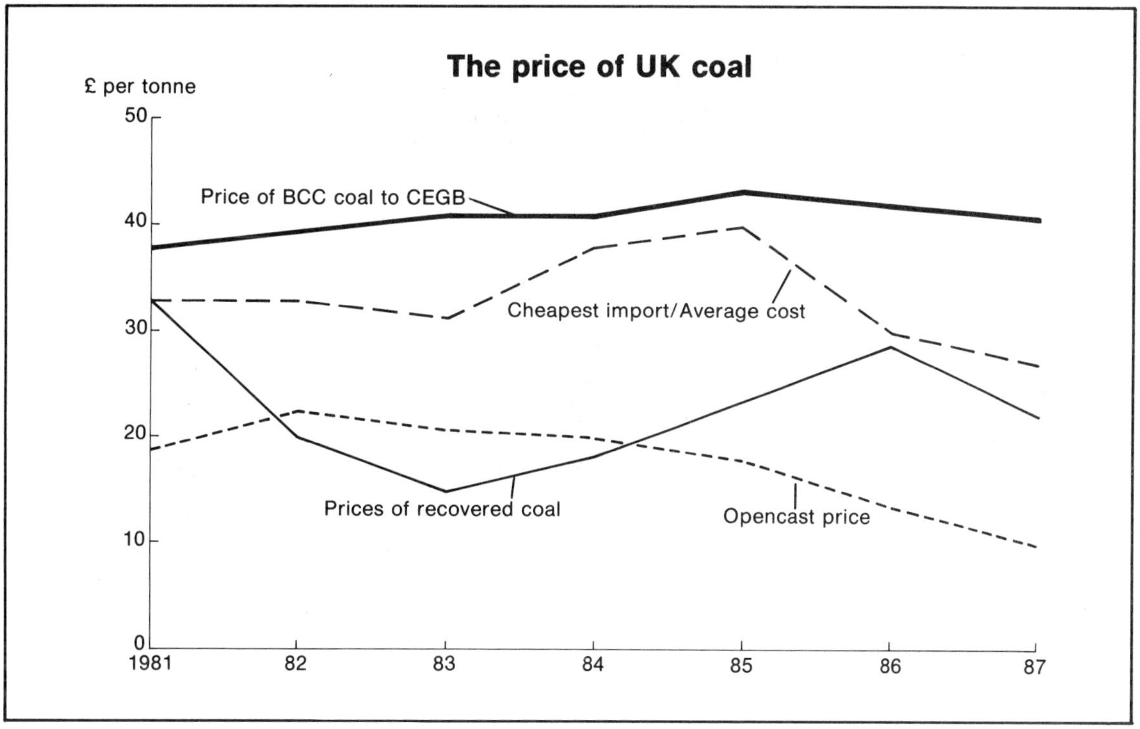

SOURCE: SUNDAY TELEGRAPH, 22 MAY 1988

a i) Compare the price of coal supplied by the British Coal Corporation with that supplied by other sources in 1987.
ii) Explain what is mean by 'opencast' and 'recovered' coal.

b British Coal is a public corporation. What does this mean?

c Give TWO reasons why you think the price of imported coal is less than the price of British coal.

d i) What do you think would be TWO benefits of privatising British Coal?
ii) Give ONE argument against privatising British Coal.

e List TWO factors that can influence the price of British coal.

JAPANESE INDUSTRY

EXERCISE 5

Study carefully the diagram below.

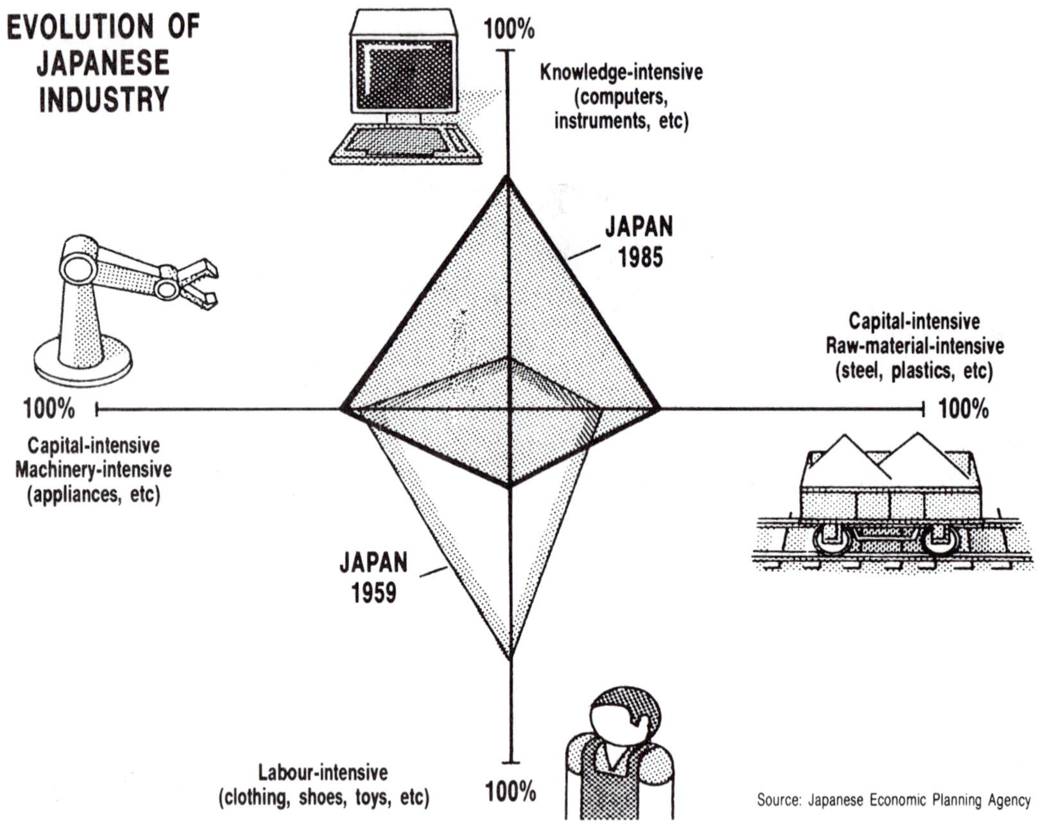

The two diamonds represent the changes in the general profile of Japanese industry from 1959 to 1985, reflected by the percentage of its extension towards specific sectors

SOURCE: THE SUNDAY TIMES, 12 JUNE 1988

a What sector of industry in Japan has experienced the greatest growth?

b In your own words explain the following terms:
i) capital-intensive industry
ii) labour-intensive industry
iii) knowledge-intensive industry

c Give TWO advantages of capital-intensive production methods over labour-intensive methods.

d What do you think is the main factor that accounts for Japanese industry's success?

IMPORTS AND EXPORTS ·1·

EXERCISE 6

Look carefully at the following picture then answer the questions.

a What does the picture suggest about the UK's balance of payments?

b i) Imports can be 'visible' or 'invisible'. What is the difference between the two terms?
ii) Give TWO examples of
1 UK invisible imports
2 UK visible imports

c Why does the UK import such a large quantity of goods?

d What could the Government do to try to discourage UK residents from buying imported goods?

IMPORTS AND EXPORTS ·2·

EXERCISE 7

Study this chart.

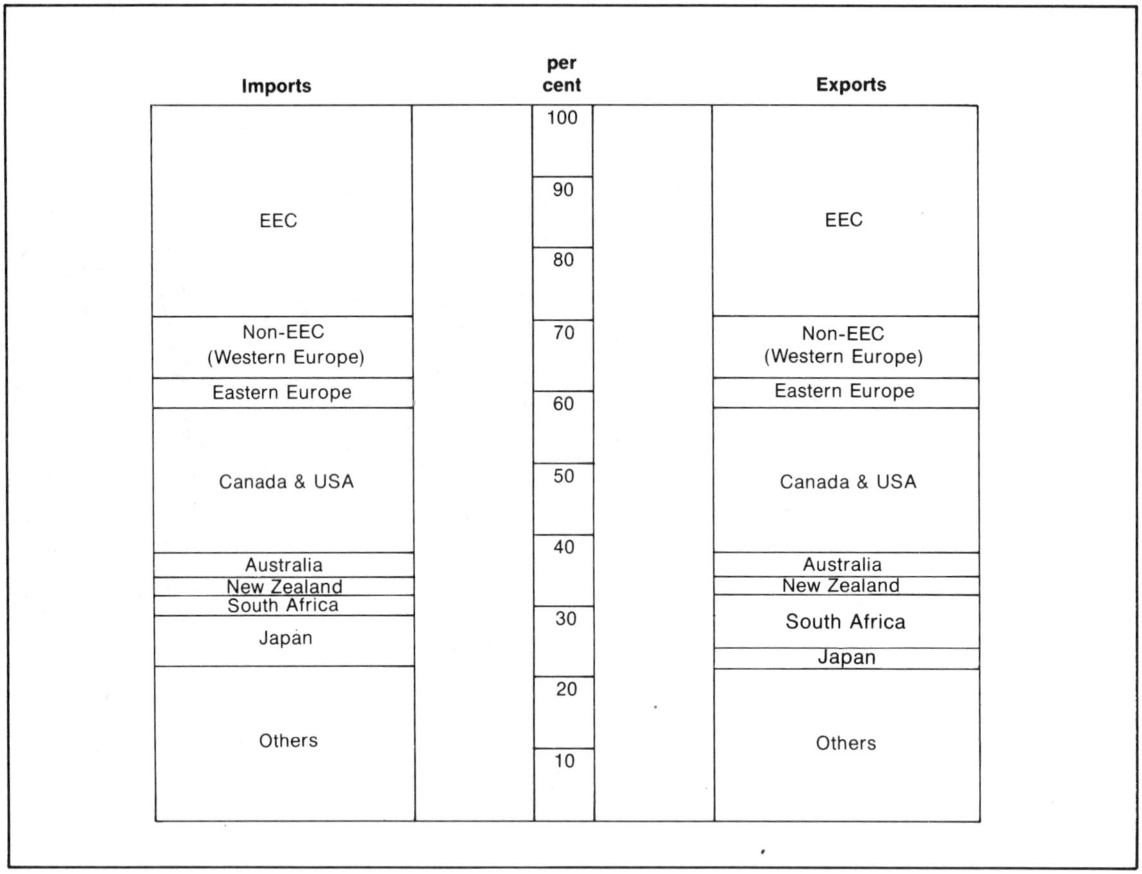

SOURCE: ECONOMIC TRENDS, 1988

a Name the member countries of the EEC.

b How do you think the pattern shown in the chart has altered over the last 50 years?

c In *percentage* terms, imports from and exports to these regions of the world appear to balance each other. However, when we look at individual countries, we find imbalances. What possible reasons are there for these imbalances in the UK's trade with
  i) Japan
  ii) South Africa?

d What are the main *types* of goods and services which Britain imports and exports?

e During 1988, Britain had a record deficit on its balance of payments. Explain why this deficit would NOT show up on a chart like the one above.

BALANCE OF PAYMENTS

EXERCISE 8

Study the graph below then answer the questions.

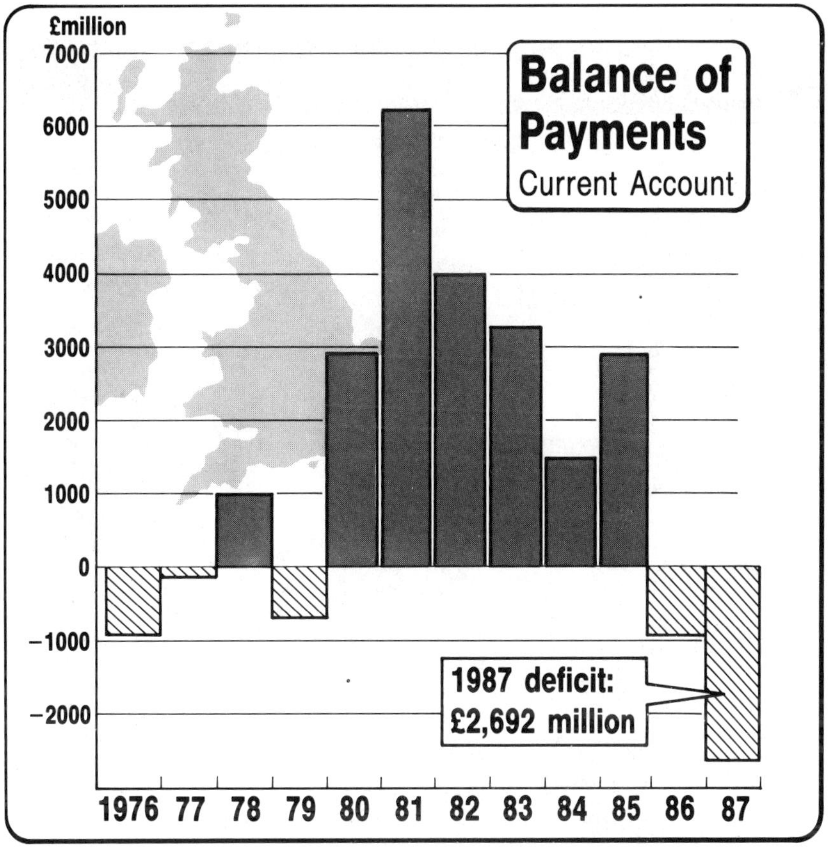

SOURCE: THE SUNDAY TIMES, 5 JUNE 1988

a The UK balance of payments is made up of two accounts. The Current Account is one, what is the other?

b Explain how you would calculate the balance of payments on Current Account.

c In 1987 there was a deficit of £2692 million. What exactly does this mean?

d From the graph, what do you know about the balance of payments on Current Account in 1981?

PRIVATISATION ·1·

Study the figures for Government proceeds from the sale of publicly owned assets, then answer the questions that follow.

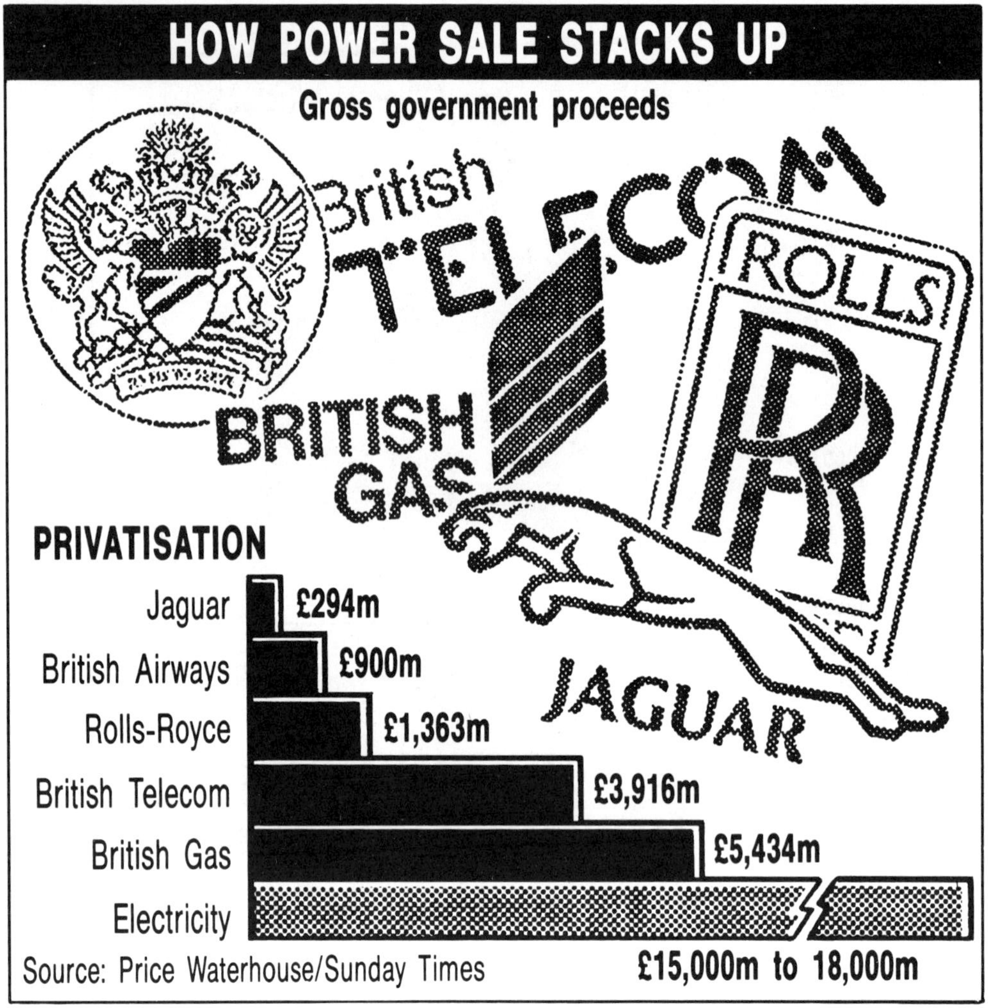

SOURCE: THE SUNDAY TIMES, 28 FEBRUARY 1988

a What do you understand by the term privatisation?

b i) Estimate, in £million, the gross Government proceeds from privatisation.
ii) Why do you think that net Government proceeds figures from privatisation might be lower than the figures in the bar graph?

c What are TWO main arguments in favour of privatising nationalised industries?

d Give ONE argument against privatising nationalised industries.

PRIVATISATION ·2·

EXERCISE 10

Study the following tables.

The nationalised industries

The list of nationalised industries which will remain in the public sector at the end of 1987–88 is as follows:-

British Coal
Electricity (England and Wales)
North of Scotland Hydro-Electric Board
South of Scotland Electricity Board
British Steel Corporation
Post Office
Girobank
British Railways Board
British Waterways Board
Scottish Transport Group
British Shipbuilders (Merchant)
Civil Aviation Authority
Water (England and Wales)
London Regional Transport

The following industries have been privatised since 1979:-

British Telecom
British Gas Corporation
British National Oil Corporation
British Airways
British Airports Authority
British Aerospace
British Shipbuilders (Warships)
British Transport Docks Board
National Freight Company
Enterprise Oil
National Bus Company (assuming privatisation completed by early 1988).

Table 1 SOURCE: ECONOMIC PROGRESS REPORT, DECEMBER 1987

Disappearing shareholders in sell-offs

Company	Sell-off dates	Number of successful share applications	Present number of shareholders
Amersham International	Feb 1982	65,000	6,077 (June 1987)
British Aerospace	Feb 1981	158,000	120,237 (Dec 1986)
	May 1985	264,000	
British Airways	Feb 1987	1,200,000	420,056 (May 1987)
British Gas	Dec 1986	4,500,000	3,111,872 (April 1987)
British Telecom	Nov 1984	2,300,000	1,417,905 (March 1987)
Britoil	Nov 1982	35,572	224,602 (Dec 1986)
	Aug 1985	450,000	
Cable & Wireless	Nov 1981	157,000	181,067 (March 1987)
	Dec 1983	35,000	
	Dec 1985	219,000	
Enterprise Oil	July 1984	13,709	13,460 (Dec 1986)
Jaguar	Aug 1984	125,000	35,749 (March 1987)

Table 2 SOURCE: LABOUR RESEARCH, SEPTEMBER 1987

a Which of the industries in Table 1 are sometimes referred to as *utilities*?

b Give reasons why the utilities are likely to be very profitable when privatised.

c What objections are there to the privatisation of utilities?

d Does Table 2 support the view that privatisation leads to wider share ownership?

e What possible explanations are there for the trend apparently shown in Table 2?

PRIVATISATION ·3·

EXERCISE 11

Read the following extract, from a letter which was sent to people who were interested in buying BP shares.

> The BP Share Offer
>
> I am writing to advise you of an important new share offer, the sale of the Government's remaining shareholding in BP.
>
> With a turnover last year of £27 billion, BP is Britain's biggest company and in a few weeks' time you will be able to apply for shares in what is likely to be Britain's biggest share offer.
>
> BP is a British company, but its activities are truly international. It is actively exploring for oil in some 25 countries, and it markets oil products as far afield as the USA, Australia, Africa, the Middle East, Europe and, of course, the UK. It is one of Europe's major petrol companies and one of the world's leading producers of animal feed.

SOURCE: BP

a What is meant by the word *turnover*?

b Besides *turnover*, what other ways are there of measuring the size of firms?

c BP is described as a 'British' company. How would you decide whether a firm is 'British' or any other nationality?

d i) Explain the difference between a public corporation and a public limited company.
ii) 'A *public* limited company belongs to the *private* sector'. Explain what this means.

e *Privatisation* in Britain has normally involved changing a public corporation into a public limited company. Explain why this did *not* apply to the case of BP.

PRIVATISATION AND DEREGULATION

EXERCISE 12

Read these newspaper extracts.

Bus fares rocket after deregulation – report

BUS FARES HAVE soared and fewer people are using the services since they were deregulated in Britain's major cities, according to a report out today.

In Merseyside, fares have risen 100 per cent since 1986 and in South Yorkshire by 238.5 per cent, it disclosed.

The report, The First Year Of Bus Deregulation, also showed that in Merseyside the number of people taking buses has fallen by almost a third.

Behaviour

The report, from the Association of Metropolitan Authorities and the Passenger Transport Executive Group, was written by Mr Bill Tyson.

An independent economist specialising in public transport, Mr Tyson said deregulation had been neither the major success the Government predicted nor a total failure.

The plus factors included a reduction in operating costs and subsidies, a high degree of competition, a constant or increased volume of service and better standards of behaviour on the roads.

The minus factors were that fewer people used the buses and "a substantial increase in real terms in fares".

SOURCE: SOUTH WALES ECHO, 2 SEPTEMBER 1988

CECIL READY TO SEND POWER BILLS SOARING

By TERRY PATTINSON, Industrial Editor

ELECTRICITY prices are set to rocket as Energy Secretary Cecil Parkinson tries to keep the industry on target for an early sell-off.

Quick privatisation plans have been threatened by breakdowns in Britain's nuclear power stations. And the cost of repairing and maintaining the five most modern A-plants has helped slash electricity profits in half.

Embarrassed power boss Lord Marshall will officially announce next week that profits plunged to £500 million last year from a record £1.1 billion the year before.

Risk

Mr Parkinson, under pressure from the City to show caution, will be left with two options if he decides to go ahead with the early sell-off.

- Force British Coal to bring its prices down still further — with the risk of more pit closures and job losses.
- Raise household electricity bills to return the industry to mega-profits and encourage investors to make a quick killing.

Mr Parkinson will be tempted to push up household power bills to bring them into line with Common Market tariffs.

But if he tries to increase charges to industry, he would find bosses in open revolt.

SOURCE: DAILY MIRROR, 24 JULY 1988

a Why is it suggested in the *Daily Mirror* extract that high electricity prices are necessary for the successful privatisation of electricity?

b What problems would higher electricity prices cause for industry?

c Why might the existence of nuclear power stations put people off buying shares in electricity?

(*continued overleaf*)

d Give reasons why it might be difficult to promote competition in the electricity supply industry.

e Distinguish between privatisation and deregulation.

f Why in the extract from the *South Wales Echo* are there no firm conclusions on whether the deregulation of the bus industry has been successful?

g The television industry is due to be deregulated in the 1990s. Write a report predicting the likely effects of this.

MONOPOLY

EXERCISE 13

Study the following diagram carefully.

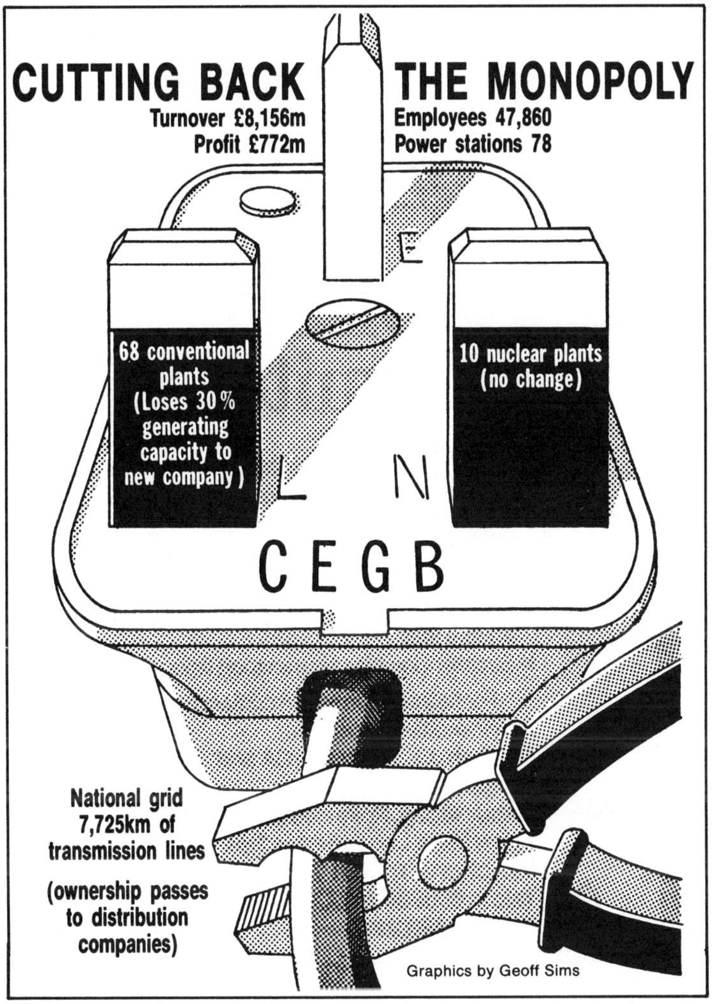

SOURCE: THE SUNDAY TIMES, 28 FEBRUARY 1988

a The diagram refers to changes which will take place when the CEGB is privatised. What do the letters CEGB stand for?

b The CEGB has a monopoly in the supply of electricity in this country.
  i) What is a monopoly?
  ii) In what ways could this affect the consumer?

c What information in the diagram could you use to measure the size of the CEGB?

d Why is it difficult to create new companies to compete with the CEGB?

DUOPOLY

EXERCISE 14

The chart shows some of the brand names used by two companies which produce detergents and allied products.

WHO WASHES WHITER?		
Procter & Gamble Ltd Newcastle-upon-Tyne	**Products**	**Lever Brothers Ltd Kingston-upon-Thames**
Fairy Liquid	WASHING-UP LIQUIDS	Sunlight, Squeezy
Ariel, Bold, Daz, Dreft, Fairy Snow, Tide	DETERGENTS	Persil, Surf, Drive
Vortex	BLEACH	Domestos
Flash	ALL-PURPOSE CLEANERS	Vigor, Handy Andy
Lenor, Bounce	FABRIC CONDITIONERS	Comfort
Camay, Fairy, Zest	TOILET SOAP	Shield, Lux, Lifebuoy, Knight's Castile
Crest, Head and Shoulders, Pampers	SOME OTHER WELL-KNOWN ITEMS	Vim, Jif

SOURCES: THE A TO Z OF UK BRAND LEADERS, 1982; UK TRADE NAMES, 1984–85

a Survey ten people who are known to you and ask them to give TWO brand names (*not* supermarket 'own brands') for each of the following:

WASHING-UP LIQUIDS
DETERGENTS
BLEACH
HOUSEHOLD CLEANERS
FABRIC CONDITIONERS
TOILET SOAP

If any brand names are mentioned which are NOT listed in the above chart, then try to find out the name of the manufacturer.

b With the help of your teacher, find out how many times each brand name was mentioned by the people interviewed by members of your class. Draw a pie chart to show the percentages of brand names mentioned which belong to Procter & Gamble, Lever Bros. and 'others'.

c People who use dishwashers need to purchase two items: dishwasher powder and 'rinse-aid' liquid.

Visit a supermarket and make a note of the brand names of these items, together with the names of their manufacturers.

d A *duopoly* exists when the market for a type of product is dominated by two large producers. On the basis of your findings, would you say that the market for detergents and allied products is a duopoly? Justify your answer.

e i) Why are products of this type the subject of heavy television advertising?

ii) At 7 o'clock one evening there is a television advertisement for Brand A toilet soap. At 8.30 the same evening there is an advertisement for Brand B. Both brands are manufactured by the same producer. Why would a firm wish to have more than one brand of a product, and why would it wish to advertise those brands, apparently in competition with each other?

FOOTLOOSE FIRMS

EXERCISE 15

Consider these definitions.

> **Localisation and Specialisation**
>
> (1) *Localised* industries contain firms which tend to be located together in certain parts of the country; *dispersed* industries are more evenly spread over the country, although they are, of course, more heavily localised where population is concentrated.
>
> (2) *Specialised* areas are heavily dependent on a narrow range of industries; *diversified* areas have a mixture of different types of industry.

a Give an example of each of the following:
- i) a localised industry
- ii) a dispersed industry
- iii) a specialised area
- iv) a diversified area

b Give reasons for the concentration/dispersal/specialisation/diversification of each of your four examples.

c Some industries have traditionally been described as 'weight losing' (e.g. steel making), or 'weight gaining' (e.g. brewing). Explain this distinction.

d Explain why a weight losing industry is likely to locate near the source of its main raw material, while a weight gaining industry is likely to locate near its market.

e Large steel mills are now located on the coast near deep water harbours, not far from the coalfields where they were originally located. Breweries are usually located in or near large cities or population centres. Use the ideas of 'weight losing' and 'weight gaining' to explain why steel works are located near the coalfields of South Wales, but breweries are NOT located on the hopfields of Kent.

f Apart from raw materials and markets, what other factors are likely to influence a firm's choice of location?

g Give reasons why many firms are 'footloose' when choosing a location.

h Newspaper production and printing was once concentrated in London's Fleet Street. These activities have now moved to a number of centres elsewhere. What changes have made this trend possible?

THE NORTH–SOUTH DIVIDE

EXERCISE 16

Study this cartoon and answer the questions.

a What is meant by the phrase 'North–South Divide'?

b One way of comparing the economies of regions such as the South East and North West is to use *unemployment rates*.

i) Make a list of FIVE other measures which you think could be used to compare regions.

ii) Give reasons why you think these measures would be useful in comparing the economic success or failure of regions.

c Give FOUR reasons why employers might prefer to locate their businesses in the South East rather than the North West.

THE SIZE OF FIRMS

EXERCISE 17

Study the following tables, which are adapted from the *Times 1000*, an annual list which gives details of the 1000 largest companies in Britain and the World, measured in several different ways. Note that *turnover* refers to the gross sales of a firm; *equity market capitalisation* is the market value of all shares issued by a company; *capital employed* is an estimate of the value of all the assets owned by a firm; and *return on capital employed* shows the profits of a firm as a percentage of its assets.

The Top 50 UK Companies, 1987 (Previous Year's Rank in Brackets)

Rank	Company Name	Main activity	Turnover (£'000)
1(1)	British Petroleum Company	Oil industry	34,247,000
2(2)	"Shell" Transport & Trading	Oil industry	22,219,000
3(3)	B.A.T. Industries	Tobacco, retailing, paper, packaging, etc.	13,623,000
4(6)	Electricity Council	Electricity suppliers	10,742,600
5(4)	Imperial Chemical Industries	Petrochemicals, pharmaceuticals, etc.	10,136,000
6(9)	S. & W. Berisford	Merchanting & commodity trading, etc.	9,695,500
7(8)	British Telecommunications	Telecommunication services	8,387,000
8(5)	Esso UK	Oil industry	8,378,600
9(10)	British Gas Corporation	Gas suppliers, etc.	7,687,200
10(7)	Shell U.K.	Oil industry	6,569,000
11(11)	Unilever	Food products, detergents, etc.	5,949,000
12(47)	National Coal Board	Coalmining	5,340,000
13(12)	Grand Metropolitan	Hotel props, milk prds., brewers, etc.	5,291,300
14(14)	General Electric Co.	Electrical engineers	5,252,600
15(19)	Dalgety	International merchants	4,909,800
16(17)	Ford Motor Co.	Motor vehicle manufacturers	4,374,000
17(33)	Hanson Trust	Industrial services & food products	4,312,000
18(16)	Phibro Salomon	Commodity brokers, etc.	4,305,022
19(21)	Marks and Spencer	General store proprietors	4,220,800
20(18)	BTR	Construction, energy & electrical, etc.	4,019,200
21(23)	J. Sainsbury	Retail distribution of food	3,857,100
22(20)	British Steel Corporation	Iron & steel mfrs, etc.	3,735,000
23(26)	Allied Lyons	Brewers, vintners, hoteliers, etc.	3,614,800
24(24)	Tesco	Multiple retailing	3,593,000
25(22)	The Rover Group	Motor vehicle manufacturers, etc.	3,412,000
26(29)	Gallaher	Tobacco, optics, pumps & valves disbn.	3,404,700
27(13)	Rio Tinto-Zinc Corporation	Mining & industrial – metals & fuel	3,343,900
28(28)	THORN EMI	Elec. & electronic eng, music, etc.	3,316,500
29(31)	British Airways	Air transportation	3,263,000
30(27)	Post Office	Mail & parcel services, etc.	3,247,500
31(30)	George Weston Holdings	Food manufacturers & distributors	3,147,600
32(34)	British Aerospace	Manufacture of aircraft, etc.	3,127,000
33(33)	Texaco	Oil industry	3,114,629
34(40)	IBM United Kingdom Holdings	Information handling eqpt. mfrs.	3,077,900
35(37)	Dee Corporation	Wholesale, retail, cash & carry distn.	2,860,384
36(41)	Beecham Group	Consumer products, pharmaceuticals, etc.	2,730,100
37(38)	Bass	Brewers	2,709,700
38(35)	Lonrho	Mining, agric., textiles, constr., etc.	2,651,000
39(98)	Guinness	Brewers	2,601,600
40(51)	ASDA-MEI Group	Dairymen, supermarket & store optrs.	2,516,600
41(36)	Conoco	Petroleum products	2,506,500
42(42)	Sears	Footwear, stores, engineering, etc.	2,480,300
43(46)	The Boots Company	Pharmaceuticals & consumer products	2,351,700
44(44)	Great Universal Stores	Stores & mail order	2,270,100
45(45)	Courtaulds	Man-made fibres, textiles, chemicals	2,261,900
46(32)	British Railways Board	Passenger railway services, etc.	2,249,300
47(86)	Saatchi & Saatchi Company	Advertising agency	2,087,000
48(43)	GKN	Steel & eng. products, fastenings, etc.	2,059,400
49(82)	Cargill UK	Commodity trading agent & principal	2,023,240
50(59)	Inchcape	International merchants	1,997,000

Table 1

The UK's top ten employers

Rank	Company	Employees	Rank in Table 1
1	British Telecommunications	233,711	7
2	National Coal Board*	199,600	12
3	Post Office*	185,293	30
4	B.A.T. Industries	176,370	3
5	British Railways Board*	173,760	46
6	Unilever	165,000	11
7	General Electric Co	164,536	14
8	Electricity Council*	132,858	4
9	Grand Metropolitan	131,493	13
10	British Petroleum Company	126,700	1

*A nationalised industry

Table 2

Equity market capitalisation

10 Highest

Rank in Table 1	Company	6 July 1987 £ million
1	British Petroleum Company	22,280.8
7	British Telecommunications	17,736.6
2	"Shell" Transport & Trading	16,484.1
80	Glaxo Holdings	12,465.6
5	Imperial Chemical Industries	9,768.0
3	B.A.T. Industries	9,450.6
19	Marks and Spencer	6,793.4
14	General Electric Co	6,346.9
17	Hanson Trust	6,305.5
20	BTR	5,508.4

Table 3

The UK's top ten capital employed

Rank	Company	Capital employed £000s	Rank in Table 1
1	Electricity Council*	38,113,800	4
2	British Petroleum Company	20,817,000	1
3	British Gas Corporation	18,438,000	9
4	"Shell" Transport & Trading	16,050,800	2
5	British Telecommunications	11,265,000	7
6	B.A.T. Industries	6,957,000	3
7	Imperial Chemical Industries	6,425,000	5
8	Hanson Trust	5,141,000	17
9	National Coal Board*	4,344,000	12
10	General Electric Co	3,521,200	14

*A nationalised industry

Table 4

The UK's top ten profit* makers

Rank	Company	Profits' £000s	Rank in Table 1
1	"Shell" Transport & Trading	2,505,000	10
2	British Telecommunications	2,219,000	7
3	British Petroleum Company	2,199,000	1
4	Esso UK	2,029,300	8
5	B.A.T. Industries	1,462,000	3
6	Imperial Chemical Industries	1,295,000	5
7	Shell U.K.	1,112,000	10
8	Electricity Council	957,200	4
9	British Gas Corporation	808,000	9
10	General Electric Co	714,400	14

*Before tax

Table 5

Return on Capital employed (UK)

20 Highest

Rank in Table 1	Company	per cent
244	Union Texas Petroleum	265.2
893	Abbott Mead Vickers	121.6
983	Kuoni Travel	121.6
840	T & S Stores	111.4
307	Robert Stephen Holdings	99.0
453	Virgin Group	91.7
1000	CMG (Computer Management Group)	88.4
242	Mercantile House Holdings	87.5
673	Charles Barker	87.2
537	Rohm and Haas (UK)	86.9
276	Amstrad	84.9
567	Ocean Exploration Co	77.1
802	National Magazine Co	77.1
344	J. Southlet (U.K.)	76.5
950	WCRS Group	72.9
433	CFF Holdings	71.1
717	DAF Trucks (GB)	70.1
326	MAI	68.2
371	Carlsberg Brewery	66.9
158	Conoco (U.K.)	64.7

Table 6

The World's Top 50 Companies			
Rank	Company	Headquarters	Sales £m
1(2)	Mitsui & Co.	Japan	76,591.5
2(3)	Mitsubishi	Japan	72,132.9
3(6)	C. Itoh	Japan	66,311.3
4(4)	General Motors	USA	63,928.9
5(8)	Sumitomo	Japan	61,006.0
6(1)	"Shell" Transport & Trading Royal Dutch Petroleum	UK Netherlands	55,547.0
7(7)	Matubeni	Japan	50,502.8
8(5)	Exxon	USA	46,623.5
9(12)	Nissho Iwai	Japan	40,152.9
10(11)	Ford Motor	USA	38,996.3
11(9)	British Petroleum	UK	34,247.0
12(13)	International Business Machines	USA	31,866.9
13(16)	Toyota Motor	Japan	28,137.0
14(10)	Mobil	USA	27,897.4
15(17)	Sears, Roebuck	USA	27,534.0
16(20)	ENI - Ente Nazionale Idrocarburi	Italy	25,381.7
17(36)	Daimler-Benz	West Germany	22,257.8
18(24)	General Electric	USA	21,894.0
19(26)	Toyo Menka Kaisha	Japan	21,684.0
20(23)	Nippon Telegraph & Telephone	Japan	21,554.5
21(21)	Hitachi	Japan	21,211.9
22(18)	American Telephone & Telegraph	USA	21,195.1
23(27)	IRI Istituto per la Ricostruzione Industriale	Italy	21,049.4
24(33)	Nichimen	Japan	20,535.7
25(14)	Texaco	USA	19,656.8
26(25)	Nissan Motor	Japan	19,590.6
27(19)	Matsushita Electric Industrial	Japan	19,368.0
28(35)	Volkswagen	West Germany	17,940.7
29(34)	Tokyo Electric Power	Japan	17,732.8
30(30)	Unilever PLC Unilever NV	UK Netherlands	17,140.0
31(22)	E.I. Du Pont de Nemours	USA	16,880.5
32(45)	Deutsche Bundespost	West Germany	16,869.2
33(32)	Philips' Lamp Holding	Netherlands	16,610.4
34(15)	Chevron	USA	16,319.0
35(31)	Siemens	West Germany	15,979.5
36(38)	Kanematsu-Gosho	Japan	15,879.5
37(—)	Philip Morris	USA	15,799.2
38(37)	Nestlé	Switzerland	15,578.3
39(47)	Mitsubishi Heavy Industries	Japan	14,957.9
40(41)	K Mart	USA	14,806.2
41(42)	Nippon Oil	Japan	14,374.6
42(49)	Toshiba	Japan	14,279.5
43(46)	Chrysler	USA	14,044.0
44(43)	Petróleos de Venezuela	Venezuela	13,869.4
45(48)	Bayer	West Germany	13,847.5
=46( )	BASF	West Germany	13,753.0
=46( )	Fiat	Italy	13,753.0
48(44)	Veba	West Germany	13,639.9
49(—)	B.A.T. Industries	UK	13,623.0
50(—)	Electricité de France	France	13,390.7

Table 7

Money Losers (UK)

Rank in Table 1	Company	Loss £000	Rank in Table 1	Company	Loss £000
25	The Rover Group	219,900	180	British Caledonian Group	2,985
148	British Shipbuilders	114,305	708	Sewgent Holdings	2,306
264	F.J.C. Lilley	45,181	386	Commodore Business Machines	2,201
72	Vauxhall Motors	31,300	666	Raybeck	1,552
360	Short Brothers	18,893	284	Amax International	1,270
614	Sinclair Research	18,226	757	Lancer Boss Group	974
647	Case Group	13,452	889	Brunning Group	940
259	Norsk Hydro (UK)	12,974	854	Rodime	908
795	Hollandsche Beton Groep (UK)	7,410	986	Seddon Diesel Vehicles	851
446	Daily Telegraph	6,686	566	Mitsubishi Electric UK	781
954	Levi Strauss (UK)	6,095	707	Consolidated Petroleum Co	731
880	Fluor Daniel	5,323	528	Citroën U.K.	684
999	Mitel Telecom	5,200	583	E.G. Cornelius & Co	603
108	Louis Dreyfus & Co	4,764	582	Geers Gross	506
702	Monarch Airlines	4,651	676	Cameron Iron Works	460
547	TRW U.K.	4,197	412	Caterpillar (U.K.)	366
816	Del Monte Foods	3,286	498	A. Monk & Co	98

Table 8

SOURCE: THE TIMES 1000 1987–88

a Why is it difficult to measure the *size* of a firm?

b Some firms are 'labour intensive' and others are 'capital intensive'. Why does this make it difficult to *compare* the sizes of firms?

c What types of activities seem to dominate Table 1? Give possible reasons why firms carrying out these activities tend to be large.

d How would you expect the UK Conservative Government's privatisation programme to affect Table 1 in the 1990s?

e Which of Tables 2, 3, 4 and 5 tend to give rankings that are similar to Table 1, and which tend to give different results? Give possible reasons for the similarities and differences.

f In Table 6, the company with the highest ranking in the *Times 1000* is Conoco UK at number 158. Look at the companies in Table 6 and you will find some familiar names. Suggest why these companies are able to provide a higher percentage return on capital employed than their larger rivals.

g Which countries dominate Table 7? Give reasons for this.

h In Table 1, BP is 'larger' than Shell; in Table 7 these positions seem to be reversed. Explain why.

i The largest money loser in Table 8 is ranked at number 25 in Table 1. Explain why it is possible to have a high turnover and yet make large losses.

CONGLOMERATES

Read the following passage.

Parents and subsidiaries

Quaker Oats is an example of a "conglomerate". A typical conglomerate comes into being over a number of years as a result of mergers between independent firms, resulting in a "holding company" or "parent company" with a number of "subsidiaries" producing between them a wide range of goods.

Quaker Oats Ltd. has its registered office in Southall, Middlesex, and is owned by the Quaker Oats Company, USA.

In 1981 its sales comprised:

Grocery products	73%
Toys	21%
Chemicals	6%

The major brand names of this conglomerate are: Quaker, Sugar Puffs (breakfast cereals); Sutherlands Spreads (meat and fish products); Chunky, Felix (pet food); Fisher Price (toys).

Cadbury-Schweppes plc is another conglomerate. Its main subsidiaries in the UK include Cadbury Ltd., Cadbury Typhoo Ltd., Jeyes Group Ltd., The Kenco Coffee Co. Ltd., Schweppes Ltd., I. Rose & Co Ltd.

It is quite possible for a subsidiary itself to act as the parent company of another subsidiary; for instance Cadbury Schweppes plc owns Cadbury Ltd. which in turn owns Kem Transport Ltd. The family tree of a conglomerate can become quite complicated.

Among Cadbury's most valuable assets are its internationally famous brand names, such as Cadbury's Dairy Milk, Crunchie, Fry's Turkish Delight, and Schweppes' Tonic Water.

SOURCE: BASED ON INFORMATION FROM THE A TO Z OF UK BRAND LEADERS, 1987

a Explain in your own words, giving examples, the meaning of each of the following terms:
  i) conglomerate
  ii) holding company
  iii) subsidiary

b Some of the firms mentioned above have the title '*plc*', others have the letters '*Ltd*' after their name. What is the difference between these terms?

c If you wished to invest in Cadbury's on the Stock Market, which company's shares would you buy?

d Mergers and takeovers between companies sometimes take place with the agreement of all involved; sometimes, however, they are more hostile and the 'victim' company resists the bid. Follow the financial news in a newspaper and write a paragraph describing the main events during a hostile takeover bid.

e There is no obvious link between pet food and children's toys. A range of products like this is said to be *diversified*. Suggest reasons why a firm might wish to diversify in this way.

f Just because a product has a brand name such as *Fry's*, *Rose's* or *Sunderland's*, we cannot assume that they are manufactured by an independent firm. They might have been at one time, but now the firm has been taken over by another. Why might a company taking over another decide to preserve the 'victim' company's brand names, instead of replacing them with its own?

MARKET SHARE • 1 •

EXERCISE 19

Study this diagram carefully. The figures on each 'bar' of the chart show the total amount spent by British consumers on the products named.

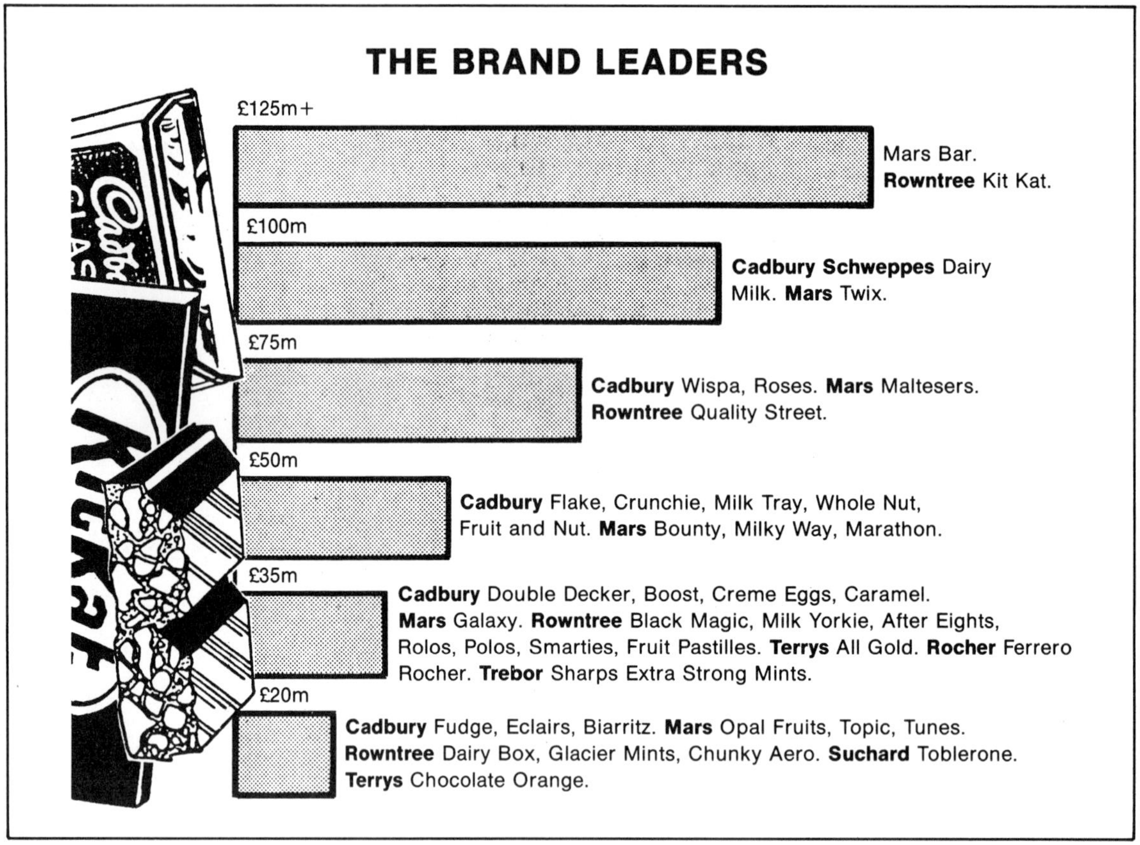

SOURCE: WESTERN MAIL, 10 MAY 1988

a i) The graph shows annual amounts spent on different brands of confectionery in the UK. Calculate the total amount of money spent on these brands of confectionery.
ii) Assuming there are 55 million people in the UK, calculate the average amount spent per person per week on confectionery made by the market leaders.

b i) Name a well-known brand of chocolate which is imported. In which country is the manufacturer located?
ii) Why have certain European chocolate manufacturers purchased shares in UK companies?

c 'Product differentiation' occurs when a manufacturer tries to create a brand image which makes its own product appear different from its rivals.
In 1986, Cadbury's introduced a new brand of chocolate called *Biarritz*. Visit a

newsagent or supermarket where chocolates are displayed and compare the appearance, price and contents of this product with others on display.

In what ways have Cadbury's attempted to *differentiate* this product? Have they been successful?

d In 1988 the Mars company introduced what was described as a 'new type of chocolate bar' called *Balisto*.

Obtain this product and examine it, paying special attention to the list of ingredients. How does it differ from the confectionery in the bar graph? If it is successful, how might it affect the market for chocolate and related goods?

MARKET SHARE ·2·

EXERCISE 20

Study carefully the information on European car market shares.

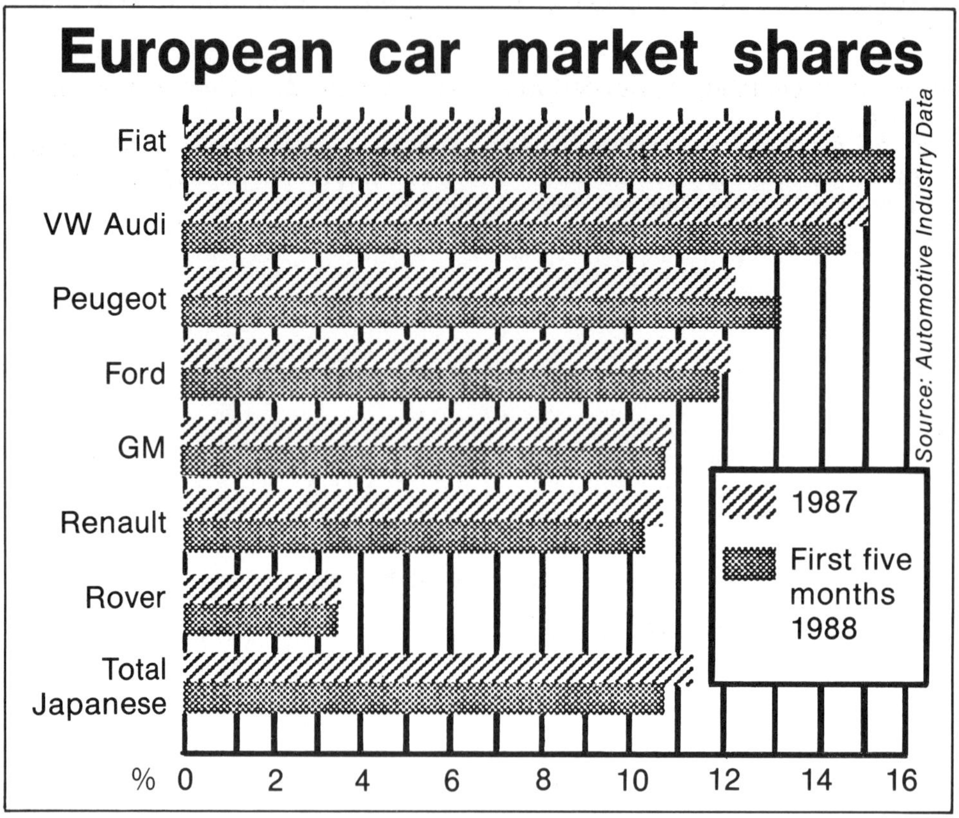

SOURCE: THE GUARDIAN, 5 JULY 1988

a i) What was the most popular make of car in Europe in 1987?
ii) What factors might account for this observation?

b i) Why are percentage shares of the market such an important aim of businesses?
ii) Name ONE other aim of businesses.

c What is the total percentage of the European car market that is supplied by the firms in the table?

d There is fierce competition amongst car manufacturers in the European car market. In what ways can firms compete with one another?

UK GROCERY CAKE

EXERCISE 21

Study the following information on the UK grocery trade.

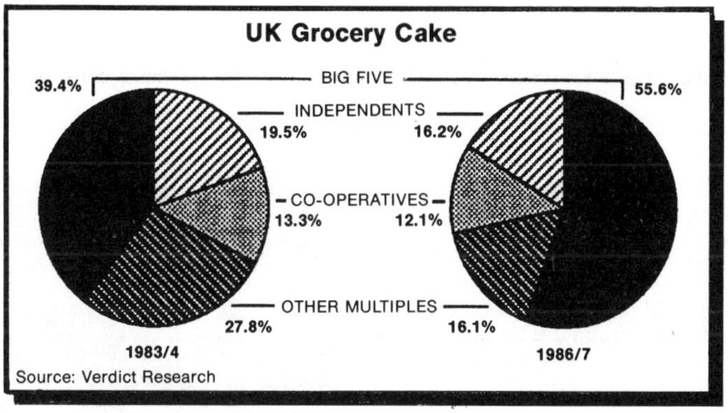

The Big Five

TESCO

SAINSBURY'S

ARGYLL GROUP PLC

ASDA

DEE

ARGYLL = SAFEWAY, PRESTO

DEE = FINE FARE, GATEWAY

SOURCE: SUNDAY TELEGRAPH, 3 APRIL 1988

a What is the most numerous type of food retail outlet in the UK?

b What do you understand by the following terms:
- i) independent
- ii) co-operative
- iii) multiple?

c What THREE advantages do multiples have over the independents?

d List THREE ways in which the independent shop can compete with the multiple.

BUSINESS FINANCE

EXERCISE 22

Examine this leaflet.

FINANCE FOR YOUR BUSINESS

Whether your needs are for day-to-day trading or to provide capital over a longer period, at Lloyds Bank our flexible approach and broad experience produce a fast, sympathetic and helpful response. Each business has different requirements; here are some examples of how we can help yours.

BUSINESS OVERDRAFT

Every business needs working capital, especially when growing, usually to bridge the gap between paying bills and receiving money from your customers. If you're a manufacturer or running a shop, you may need to buy extra material or stock to meet large orders or high seasonal demands.

Our Business Overdraft provides short-term finance and can be agreed very simply. You can use as much of the facility as you need, paying interest only on the amount acutally borrowed.

And unlike other banks, we charge interest monthly, which makes budgeting easier for you.

a Explain the differences between an overdraft and a loan.

b What do bankers mean by *security*?

LLOYDS BANK BUSINESS LOANS

Should you need more than an overdraft, one of our range of Business Loans could be for you. For example, if you're buying a fixed asset for the business - office equipment, machinery, vehicles - we'd recommend spreading the cost over several years rather than stretch your immediate cash resources.

We can provide up to 100 per cent of the purchase price, whatever your needs may be. If you are considering property purchase, see our Business Mortgages.

You'll always find our interest rates competitive, and the interest itself is normally a tax-deductible expense for businesses.

SMALL BUSINESS LOAN

Provides between £1,000 and £15,000 for any business purpose. Repayable over 1-5 years, with a fixed interest rate and monthly repayments so you always know where you are with budgeting. We make it simple, straightforward and easy to arrange.

BUSINESS LOAN

For amounts over £15,000, and with repayment periods of up to 30 years. Its exceptional flexibility includes a wide range of interest and repayment options that can be tailored to your business needs. For example, capital payments can be postponed during the first two years - perhaps until your new purchase is producing income; repayments can be linked to an endowment assurance policy; monthly or quarterly repayments are available; interest can be fixed or variable - and reviewed every five years.

FRANCHISE BUSINESS LOAN

This increasingly popular way of setting up in your own business may demand capital investment. We offer advice and provide finance quickly - as soon as you're accepted by a proven franchisor - on the same basis as our business loans.

BUSINESS LOAN REPAYMENT INSURANCE - FOR COMPLETE PEACE OF MIND

This special policy is available with most types of business loan. It can also apply to our commercial mortgages if used for purposes such as building extensions and refurbishment projects (but it is not available if the loan is for the purchase of freeholds or land).

It protects your business (or your family) at a competitive cost, covering loans of up to £50,000 and up to 10 years. It meets loan repayments on an insured person's disability through illness or accident until recovery (up to 24 months), and clears the outstanding balance on death.

You can have the premium added to your loan at the outset and included in your repayments, which saves you having to find an additional lump sum, and enables you to concentrate your cash resources where they are most useful.

SMALL FIRM LOAN GUARANTEE SCHEME

We support the Government guarantee scheme, which helps provide finance for businesses that have viable business plans but may lack the security of capital needed to achieve their aims. This type of loan is available from as little as £2,000 and up to £75,000.

SOURCE: LLOYDS BANK SMALL BUSINESS SERVICES

c Suppose you wished to set yourself up in business as a producer of racing cycles. Which of the types of finance shown on this leaflet would probably be the most suitable to get you started? Justify your answer.

d Make a list of other banking services which would be useful to a small or medium-sized business.

CURRENT ACCOUNTS

Study the newspaper article and the chart.

Current account war spreads

By Patrick Hosking
Banking Correspondent

MIDLAND BANK and Lloyds Bank yesterday fired the opening salvoes in what promises to be a costly and long-running war to keep existing personal account-holders and poach new customers from their rivals. The key weapon is the offer of interest-bearing current accounts.

Midland unveiled three revamped branded accounts, each offering interest on in-credit balances from 20 February. Lloyds swiftly retaliated, bringing forward by 24 hours the launch of its new interest-bearing current account Classic, available from today, and increasing the interest rates it had planned to offer.

The other two main clearers are not far behind. Barclays said yesterday it would be announcing details of its interest-bearing accounts early in February. National Westminster would only say it would be making an announcement shortly.

Also yesterday the Co-operative Bank, a pioneer of interest-bearing accounts re-entered the fray, raising the interest rate on that part of Cheque & Save account balances above £2,500 from 8.5 to 9 per cent.

Meanwhile, Save and Prosper, the unit trust group with 50,000 banking customers, abolished its £2-a-month bank charges for current accounts in credit.

The moves are further evidence of a growing war for current account customers among banks and building societies. But they herald far more radical changes to come. According to Dr John Wrigglesworth, building societies analyst with stockbroker Phillips & Drew, this is just the start of an era of much greater competition among the banks and societies.

He said yesterday: "I see much longer opening hours, including Sunday opening. I see free glasses being offered, like petrol stations, and even bingo . . .

"The Alliance & Leicester [building society] is already offering free cameras to customers who pay their salaries directly into their accounts."

In the shorter term, however, the payment of interest is likely to have a depressing effect on the banks' figures. Midland expects the move to cost a net £15m in its first year, rising to £40m by 1991. Lloyds is more circumspect, but privately believes the cost of its scheme will be greater.

All the banks, however, will ensure that the switch to paying interest is as slow as possible. None is expected to pay interest to customers with existing current accounts.

It will be up to each customer actively to request a switch to the newly-created account. Inertia, apathy and ignorance are on the side of the banks.

Nevertheless, the Midland expects between 15 and 17 per cent of its 4.5 million ordinary current account holders — 675,000 or more — to switch to one of its three interest-bearing accounts this year. It forecasts that the proportion will rise to 48 per cent by 1991.

The new terms of Lloyds' Classic account will be 4.5 per cent interest paid on balances greater than £1 and 6.5 per cent above £500. The rates provisionally envisaged when the account was announced last October, before the most recent base rate rise, were respectively 4 and 6 per cent.

The Midland package — under the brand names Vector, Orchard and Meridian — offers interest rates ranging from 5 to 8 per cent.

They are not strictly comparable with one another or with rival accounts because of different fixed rate charges, different interest-earning bands and a variety of optional extras.

The revamped Vector account, which already has 150,000 customers, pays a flat rate of 7 per cent on in-credit balances, offers a free overdraft up to £250 but charges a fixed monthly fee of £10.

The Orchard account offers 5 per cent interest on the first £250, rising to a top rate of 7.5 per cent on balances above £1,000. The Meridian, "for wealthier individuals", pays rates from 6.5 per cent to a top rate of 8 per cent for balances above £2,000.

Midland, which has pursued a distinctive marketing strategy of heavily branding its products, also launched its first Visa credit card, to be called Indigo.

The trigger for the banks' rush to offer more attractive current account terms has been the success of building societies in winning new customers, either with card-based current accounts or, in the case of Abbey National and Nationwide Anglia, with cheque-book-based accounts.

Nationwide Anglia launched its Flex Account in May 1987. It last stated it had 800,000 customers and the figure is now believed to be closer to one million.

Abbey National says it has 800,000 account-holders for its current account, 550,000 of them joining since March.

Those two building societies alone have therefore carved out a 5 per cent share of the 32 million current account market in less than two years. The banks are understandably worried.

SOURCE: THE INDEPENDENT, 4 JANUARY 1989

HOW THE DIFFERENT CURRENT ACCOUNTS LINE UP

Bank/Building Society	Charges when in credit	Interest on accounts	Charges if overdrawn	Arranged overdrafts	Unofficial overdrafts
National Westminster	None. Waived if av bal is £500 qtr	None	28p all debits; £3 qtrly fee	3-7% over base rate	25% (Apr 27.4%)
Barclays	None. Waived if av bal is £500 qtr	None	29p all debits; £3 qtrly fee	3-7% over base rate	15% over base rate
Midland	None	None	30p (27p direct debits); £3 qtrly	19.2%	Apr 26.2%
(Vector)	£10 a mth	3% net	None	Over £250 1.5% a mth (Apr 19.5%)	Manager's discretion
Lloyds	None. Waived if av bal is £500 qtr	None	25p all debits; £1 mthly fee	1.5% a mth (Apr 19.5%)	Apr 29.8%
TSB	None. Waived if av bal is £500 qtr	None	29p all debits; £3 qtrly fee	3-5% over base rate	13.5% over base rate
Nationwide Anglia	None	1.5%-3.5% net	None	1.25 or 1.75% (Secured/un-secured) a mth	2.5% a mth (Apr 34.4%)
Abbey National	None	3.5% net	None	1.5% a mth (Apr 19.5%)	2.2% a mth (Apr 29.8%)

SOURCE: THE GUARDIAN, 29 MAY 1988

a i) If a current account is *overdrawn*, what does this mean?
ii) What is the difference between an *arranged* and *unofficial* overdraft?

b Compare the information in the chart with that in the newspaper article, and note the rapid changes that have taken place during the time between the publication of the two. Why did the business for current accounts become so much more competitive during 1988–89?

c Most commercial banks belong to the clearing system. With the help of a simple diagram explain how this system provides an *aid* to the business of banking.

d Briefly explain how the Bank of England *controls* the business of banking.

MORTGAGES

Examine this illustration.

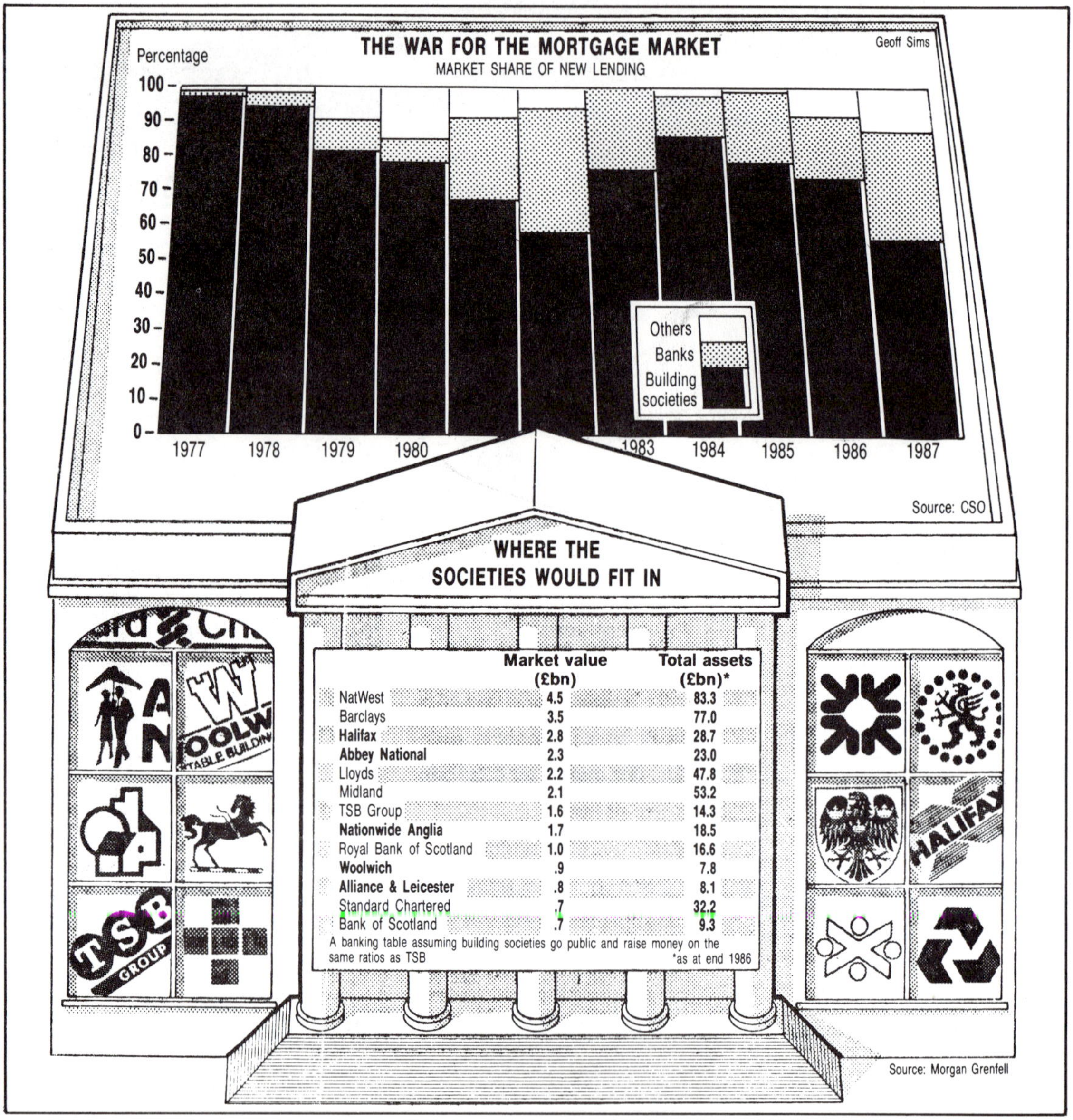

	Market value (£bn)	Total assets (£bn)*
NatWest	4.5	83.3
Barclays	3.5	77.0
Halifax	2.8	28.7
Abbey National	2.3	23.0
Lloyds	2.2	47.8
Midland	2.1	53.2
TSB Group	1.6	14.3
Nationwide Anglia	1.7	18.5
Royal Bank of Scotland	1.0	16.6
Woolwich	.9	7.8
Alliance & Leicester	.8	8.1
Standard Chartered	.7	32.2
Bank of Scotland	.7	9.3

A banking table assuming building societies go public and raise money on the same ratios as TSB

*as at end 1986

SOURCE: THE SUNDAY TIMES, 27 MARCH 1988

a The illustration contains the company logo or symbol of a number of financial institutions. Keep an eye open for advertisements over the next few weeks, and match each symbol with the name of the relevant institution.

b You will have noticed that the market for mortgages has become very competitive. Why do the commercial banks wish to expand in the mortgage market?

c Why are mortgages important
i) to families
ii) to businesses?

d The 'price' of a mortgage is the interest rate which borrowers are charged on repayments. Visit the local branches of some of the banks and building societies which are mentioned in the illustration. Make a note of their mortgage rates. Do these rates differ very much? Give possible reasons for your answer.

e Banks are becoming more like building societies, and building societies are becoming more like banks. State one major advantage and disadvantage to the customer of this trend.

CREDIT CARDS

EXERCISE 25

Look at this information.

Our name here means that your Visa card is issued by Chase Manhattan Bank, as a principal member of the Visa organisation.

Your personal Visa number. Use it whenever you have any queries regarding your account.

Your card expires on the last day of the month shown. A new card will be sent to you automatically before that date, assuming that your account remains in good standing.

Your name identifies the card as your own and is checked against your signature as an added security precaution.

SOURCE: CHASE MANHATTAN BANK

a There are four major card organisations: Mastercard, Visa, American Express and Diners International. Most banks and building societies issue cards in the name of either Mastercard or Visa. Name ONE Mastercard credit card and THREE Visa cards.

b What are the main advantages and disadvantages of credit cards
i) to the cardholder
ii) to the retailer?

c Why would a credit card be particularly useful to a business person who does a lot of travelling?

d Imagine you are on holiday in Spain and you see an expensive leather bag you would like to purchase. You decide to use your credit card. Describe the stages in the credit card system, starting with the decision to buy, and finishing with your final payment.

NATIONAL GIROBANK

EXERCISE 26

Look at this illustration.

A massive customer base and the largest retail banking network in the country are the major attractions for the private sector in the sale of Girobank.

SOURCE: THE OBSERVER, 12 JUNE 1988

a What organisation runs the National Girobank?

b Explain in your own words the two main advantages which Girobank has over the other banks. Can you think of any other advantages?

c For what reason does the illustration suggest the Government might be keen to turn Girobank into a public limited company?

SUPPLY AND DEMAND ·1·

EXERCISE 27

Look at this graph, which shows the general pattern of output of apples in country X throughout the year.

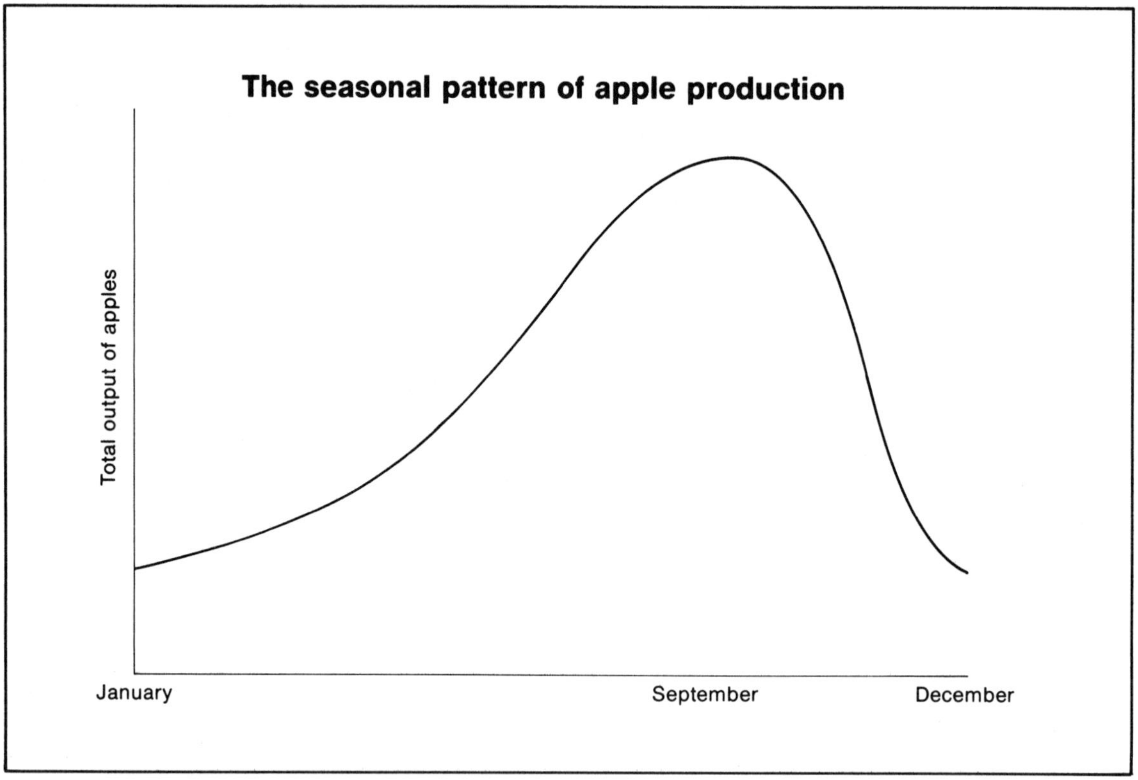

a Assuming demand remains the same throughout the year, in which month are apples likely to have
   i) the highest prices
   ii) the lowest prices?

b In which month are wholesalers likely to be
   i) building up their stocks
   ii) selling from their stocks?

c Explain carefully how wholesalers help to *stabilise* the price of apples.

SUPPLY AND DEMAND ·2·

EXERCISE 28

Read this newspaper article.

SLIPPED DISCS

Pop's gold award loses its lustre

HITS

BING Crosby, with White Christmas, was the first star to sell a million. The Beatles had four million-plus discs. And the last to reach the magic figure was Jennifer Rush.

MISSES

SINGERS Yazz, Kylie Minogue and Cliff Richard all had huge hits. But none got anywhere near a million. The pop single, it seems, is doomed to fade away

EXCLUSIVE
by DAVID HANCOCK

THE Gold Disc, glittering target of pop stars for decades, is losing its shine.

Because of falling sales, a performer now needs to sell only 400,000 copies of a single, instead of half a million, to qualify.

The more prestigious Platinum Disc is devalued even further. It drops from a million copies to a mere 600,000.

And the Silver Disc tumbles, too — from 250,000 to 200,000.

The change by the British Phonographic Industry took place, quietly, on January 1.

It amounts to an admission that the old-fashioned pop single is on the way out.

There has not been a million-selling single in Britain since Jennifer Rush's The Power of Love in 1985.

Yazz squeezed 710,000 out of The Only Way Is Up last year and Kylie Minogue could only manage to notch up 650,000 with I Should Be So Lucky.

Value

Even this Christmas, with its traditional surge in single sales, Cliff Richard's Mistletoe And Wine barely passed that figure.

It's a far cry from the heady days of the Seventies, when sales reached 90 million a year.

Paul McCartney's Mull Of Kintyre passed two million with ease at Christmas in 1977.

Peter Crompton of the Media Research and Information Bureau explains: "It is simply a matter of price.

"At £1.60 or more, a single isn't good value when you can buy the whole album for £5.99.

"Singles sales have dropped from 77 million in 1984 to just over 60 million last year. That is an amazing fall."

Single compact discs are taking over from the seven-inch vinyl record.

There have been 44 million-selling singles in Britain since Bing Crosby started the trend in 1942 with White Christmas. The Group to collect the most was the Beatles with She Loves You, Can't Buy Me Love, I Want To Hold Your Hand and A Hard Day's Night.

SOURCE: DAILY MIRROR, 4 JANUARY 1989

a Why has the demand for *singles* fallen?

b Do you think that the *overall* demand for the products of the Phonographic Industry has risen or fallen over the years? Give reasons.

c What is meant in business by a *loss leader*? To what extent might singles be regarded as *loss leaders*?

d Select a suitable sample of your acquaintances. Design a questionnaire and survey the demand for singles. Find out to what extent the quantity of singles demanded would increase if prices were lowered.

e Imagine that you are a consultant engaged by the Phonographic Industry. Write a report on the future of the market for singles.

TELEVISION ADVERTISING ·1·

EXERCISE 29

The chart shows a list of advertisements on Yorkshire Television at selected times on a Friday, Saturday and Sunday in 1981 (note that this was before the time of 'breakfast' television).

Chronological list of commercials, Yorkshire Television, week-ending 18 Oct. 1981

A	B	C	D
Friday			
K TEL HOOKED/CLASSICS	1225	10	156
L MARX SUPERSTAR3000	1226	30	156
BERWICK MUSICAL BIRD	1226	30	156
VALLANCES	1227	30	138
HAMILTON ROSS	1227	30	138
PERSIL	1228	40	138
BATCHELORS CUP/SOUP	1228	10	138
LENTHERIC MYSTIQUE	1228	20	138
CARNATION COFFEEMATE	1229	10	138
NEW STORK SB	1256	40	225
MR KIPLING MACAROONS	1256	30	225
ENGLISH CHEESE	1257	30	242
PURA SOLID VEG OIL	1257	40	242
BOVRIL PASTE	1258	30	242
WHISKAS CAT FOOD	1259	40	251
* * *			
Saturday			
ETCH A SKETCH	1027	30	121
NORTHERN UPHOLSTERY	1027	30	121
SMITHS SQUARE CRISPS	1056	40	104
PALTY STAR WARS	1057	30	112
LEWIS STORE	1057	7	112
PALTY STOCKCAR	1121	15	147
BURTONS PIGLETS	1122	30	138
BERWICK BATHTIME FUN	1122	30	138
PALTY TINY TEARS	1123	30	138
ALTON TOWERS	1123	15	138
PETER PAN FRUSTRATN	1123	15	138
ACTION HOVERCRAFT	1124	15	138
CBS SHAKY LP	1141	30	130
L MARX SUPERSTAR3000	1141	30	130
PALTY ACTION MAN	1142	20	121
IWS KNITWEAR	1142	20	121
STRIPES	1143	30	130
PETER PAN OTHELLO	1143	30	130
ALTON TOWERS	1154	15	147
HORNBY RAILWAY	1154	40	147
PALTY STOCKCAR	1155	15	147
PETER PAN OTHELLO	1155	20	147
IDEAL COLORFORMS	1155	20	147
ACTION CRPS/UP LADDR	1155	40	147
* * *			
SUN	1926	20	719
IMPERIAL LEATHER SOAP	1926	30	719
ANTI SMOKE	1927	30	719
CADBURY DOUBLE DECKR	1927	20	719
METTOY CORGI TOYS	1927	30	719
FLETCHERS BREAD	1928	20	728
CBS SHAKY LP	1941	30	675
QUEENSWAY WAREHOUSES	1941	20	675
DAILY STAR	1942	40	658
BROOKE BOND DIVI TEA	1942	30	658
ROWNTREE DRIFTER	2000	30	658
GOLDENLAY EGGS	2001	30	649
QUANTAS AIRLINE SRVC	2001	30	649
DAILY STAR	2020	40	684
MORNING FRESH LIQUID	2021	30	684
CHEF BOX SOUPS	2021	30	684
MARS TUNES	2022	30	684
MMB CREAM CAKES	2022	15	684
PIONEER HI-FI	2036	30	719
C&B COOK IN THE POT	2037	30	693
* * *			
Sunday			
SUBARU MV PCKUP 1800	1141	10	69
CHANDOR HERBICIDE	1141	30	69
AVADEX BW HERBICIDE	1142	30	69
ARELON LIQUID	1142	15	69
HOECHST HOEGRASS	1142	10	69
FF 4006 CHEMICALS	1143	20	69
FLASH FLOOR CLEANER	1143	30	69
LENOR FABRIC SOFTENR	1155	45	78
WIGFALLS	1156	30	78
BURGESS ANIMAL FOODS	1156	20	78
GILPINS	1156	15	78

Key
A = Advertiser
B = Time
C = Duration (seconds)
D = Homes viewing (000s)

SOURCE: BROADCASTERS' AUDIENCE RESEARCH BOARD (BARB) LTD

a Is it possible to identify the type of viewer which the advertisements are aimed at during
   i) Friday lunchtime
   ii) Saturday morning
   iii) Saturday evening
   iv) Sunday morning?

   Give reasons for your answer.

b During which of these time spots would you expect it to be most expensive for advertisers to buy airtime? Why?

c How has the pattern of output of TV programmes changed during the 1980s? What effects, if any, do you think these changes have had on advertising?

TELEVISION ADVERTISING ·2·

EXERCISE 30

Read the following extract carefully.

Right on target to catch the viewers

ADWATCH by Sue Stoessl

THE MAIN television set in almost all homes is in the living room, where it is still watched by family groups rather than people on their own. About 70 per cent of households watch the TV together during the average evening, which means that programmes have to appeal to people across generations, both sexes and a wide range of interests.

The two major channels, BBC 1 and ITV, therefore, aim much of their output at mass family audiences. Almost everyone who lives in a household with a television set watches something on BBC or ITV every week. The average person spends about 22 hours a week watching ITV and BBC 1. This leaves Channel 4 and BBC 2 with up to five hours of viewing to share between them. They can make inroads into the major channels' time only by showing mass audience appeal programmes — mainly sport.

Many BBC 2 and Channel 4 programmes are targeted narrowly: a Channel 4 music programme will be of interest to connoisseurs of jazz or classical music or pop, not to people who have only a general interest in music. Comedy programmes like *The Comic Strip Presents* on Channel 4, or *The Young Ones* on BBC 2, have little appeal to older viewers. To comply with the broadcasting act that brought it into being, Channel 4 tries to cater for tastes and interests not served elsewhere.

Targeting at viewers has evolved during the 1980s, and with it the concept of advertising to special groups. Many magazines have limited rather than mass appeal, and television can meet the same needs and attract the same advertisers. The *Chart Show* on Channel 4, for instance, features pop videos and is made for younger viewers: 54 per cent of its audience is under 25.

The programme must also be scheduled for when the target audience can watch and get control of the set. Between 6 and 7pm on a Friday has become a young people's viewing on Channel 4 — before they go out and while the older generation is generally otherwise occupied. The last year's development of late evening and night-time television is also catering for young tastes; after 11pm nearly half the audience is under 35 and can be programmed for very specifically.

In contrast, the quiz show *Countdown* draws more than half its audience from the over 65s who are at home on weekday afternoons between 4.30 and 5pm. This programme might appeal across the age groups but it is scheduled against children's programmes on ITV and BBC 1.

Other programmes on Channel 4 cater for particular interests and hobbies: business affairs, fishing, gardening, history, quilting. In the early days of Channel 4, many people scoffed when the first quilting programme was scheduled. It took time to explain that there was a place for such special interest programmes even if they only appealed to relatively few people. Now this idea is accepted and targeting is seen as a device for placing advertisements in the right editorial environment.

The author is Head of Marketing, Channel 4.

SOURCE: THE INDEPENDENT, 24 AUGUST 1988

a Explain in your own words what is meant by the *targeting* of advertising.

b Why has it always been easier to target magazine advertising than television advertising?

c The extract mentions that 54 per cent of the audience of the *Chart Show* is under the age of 25. If you were a TV executive, how would you go about obtaining information of this kind?

d What developments have made it easier for TV advertisements to be targeted?

e Why would more efficient targeting reduce the amount which manufacturers have to spend on advertising?

f How might the introduction of cable and satellite television affect the ability of advertisers to *target* their audiences?

SLOGANS AND BRAND NAMES

EXERCISE 31

Read these advertising slogans.

If you see
Sid, tell him

Gotta Lotta Bottle

Refreshes the part others cannot reach

The Listening Bank

THE MINT WITH THE HOLE

Have a break have a?

The Bank that likes to say "Yes"

This is the age of the?

I bet he drinks . . .

. . . washes whiter

A hazelnut in every bite

I'm with the?

9 out of 10 cats prefer . . .

That will do nicely

You can eat between meals
without ruining your appetite

Beanz Meanz?

. . . helps
you work
rest and
play

. . . hands
that do
dishes . . .

a Match each of these slogans with its brand name.

b Millions of pounds are spent each year on advertising. Pick out one of the slogans which in your opinion represents a good investment on the part of the advertiser and explain why.

c Choose one of the following products:
i) a new family car to compete with the Ford Escort
ii) a sun tan lotion
iii) a breakfast cereal
Give the product a brand name and devise a slogan suitable for television and/or press advertising.

d i) Describe the section of the population (e.g. working women, teenagers) at which your advertisement in (c) is aimed, and explain how this influenced your choice of brand name and slogan.
ii) What sort of *image* are you trying to create for your product? In what ways is your product *differentiated* from its competitors?

e The brand name *Jif* is used by two separate producers. One uses it for a bathroom cleaner, the other for lemon juice in a plastic container.
i) Give likely reasons why the name *Jif* is thought of as being suitable for each product.
ii) Why might it be undesirable (or even dangerous) for these two products to carry the same name?

f Look at this list:

SELLOTAPE	TARMAC
HOOVER	MACKINTOSH
BIRO	THERMOS
WALKMAN	ASTROTURF
PORTAKABIN	COLA
TANNOY	FILOFAX
JCB	XEROX

What do names of this type suggest to you about the importance of brand images in our society?

COSTS

Look at the following chart and graph carefully.

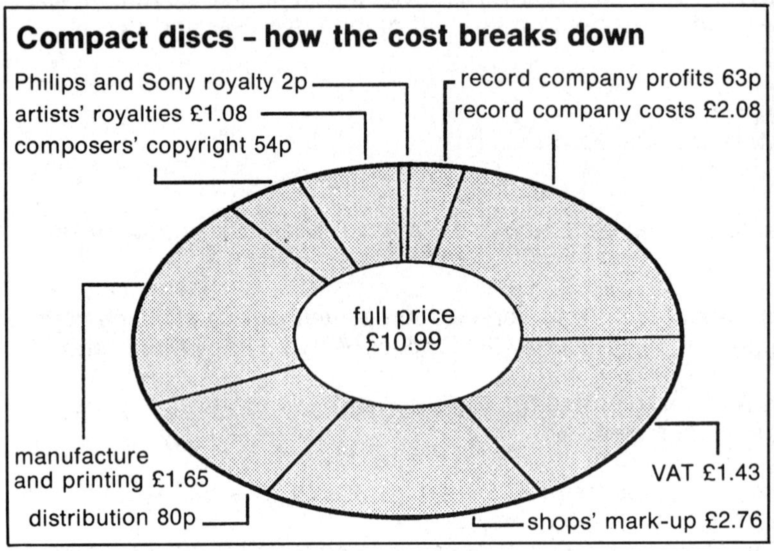

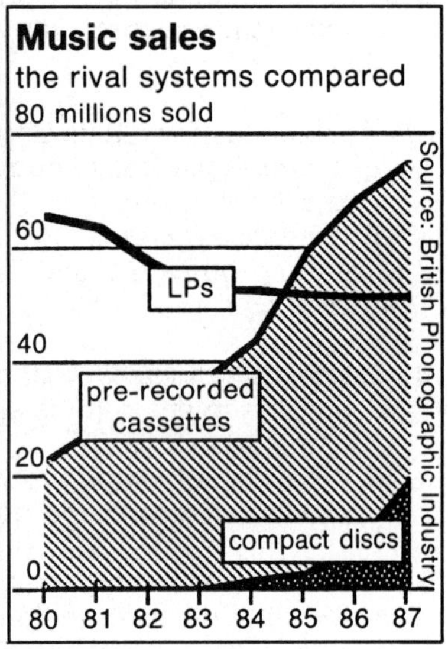

SOURCE: THE GUARDIAN, 2 MAY 1988

a What is a royalty?

b Calculate the percentage of the total price accounted for by Value Added Tax.

c i) What has happened to the sale of LPs since 1980?
ii) What might account for this trend?

d Explain the following terms:
i) composers' copyright
ii) shops' mark-up
iii) distribution costs

e i) Explain the difference between fixed costs and variable costs.
ii) Place each of the cost items given in the chart under the following headings: *fixed costs* and *variable costs*.

f What factors affect the demand for compact discs?

TURNOVER OF SELECTED INDUSTRIES

EXERCISE 33

Study the following chart carefully.

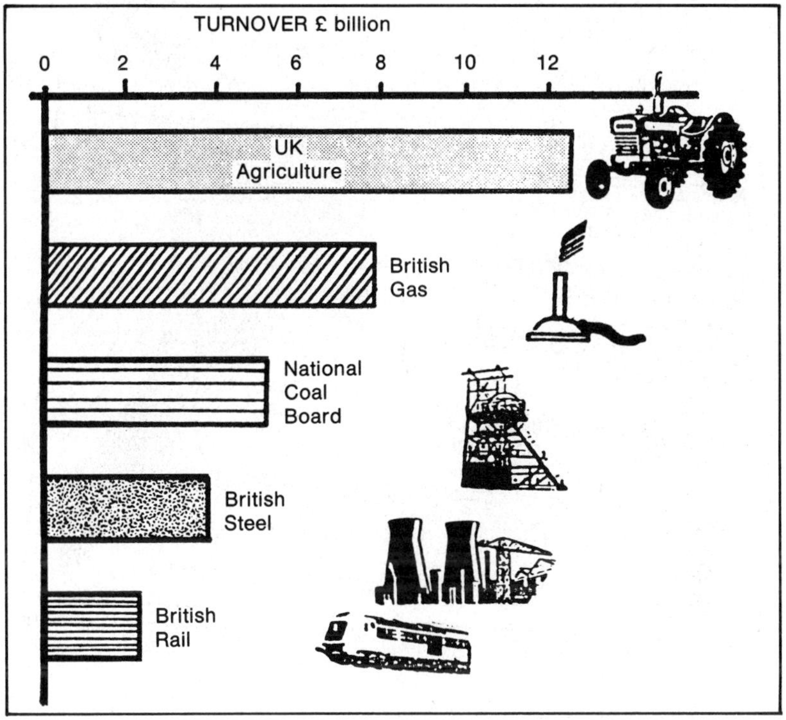

SOURCE: WESTERN MAIL, 23 JUNE 1988

a What is another term meaning *turnover*?

b Do you think the industry with the largest turnover is necessarily the most profitable? Explain your answer.

c Why do you think that the UK agriculture industry's turnover is so much greater than that of British Gas?

d i) What do the letters 'CAP' stand for?
ii) How has it affected the UK agriculture industry?

e A certain UK primary industry with greater turnover than agriculture is not shown on the chart. What is it?

PROFITS

EXERCISE 34

Examine the information about P & O.

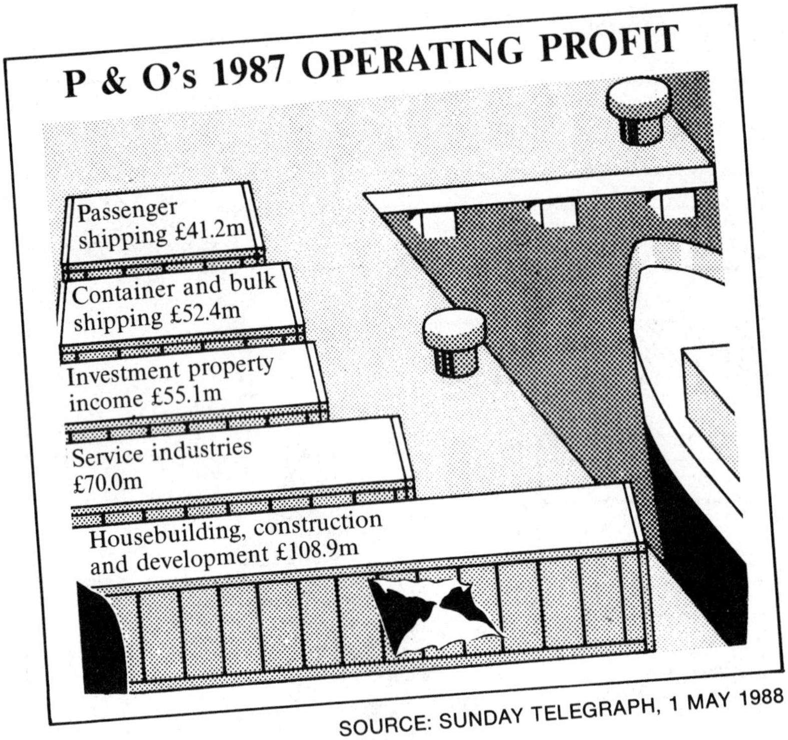

SOURCE: SUNDAY TELEGRAPH, 1 MAY 1988

a What type of business organisation is P & O?

b i) What is the most profitable operation of the P & O company?
ii) Give TWO reasons which might account for this fact.

c What do you think happens to the profits that P & O earns?

d Operating profit is also known as gross profit. Explain the difference between gross profit and net profit.

PROFIT AND LOSS ·1·

EXERCISE 35

Study the information on the Banks' Balance Sheet carefully, then answer the questions.

Banks' Balance Sheet

	BARCLAYS	LLOYDS	MIDLAND	NATWEST
1987 Results	£339m Profit	£248m Loss	£505m Loss	£704m Profit
Total Assets Dec 31	£ 87.7bn	£44.9bn	£48.4bn	£87.0bn
Share Price Now	479p	265p	398p	568p
Change on Week	+14p	+7p	no change	+20p

SOURCE: SUNDAY TELEGRAPH, 28 FEBRUARY 1988

a Draw a bar graph to represent the 1987 figures on profit/loss for the Big Four banks.

b The total assets figure for Barclays bank is £87.7 billion. Give some examples of the assets that make up this figure.

c i) Banks are public limited companies. Explain what this means.
ii) How are the share prices of the Banks related to the profit/loss situation?

d In your own words, explain how banks make a profit.

e On any balance sheet there is a list of assets and liabilities. What are the banks' liabilities?

f A major reason for the losses shown in the chart is the non-payment of loans by Third World countries. Explain:
i) why Third World countries need bank loans;
ii) why lending to Third World countries is a high-risk business.

PROFIT AND LOSS ·2·

EXERCISE 36

Study carefully the following statistics for the Rover Group.

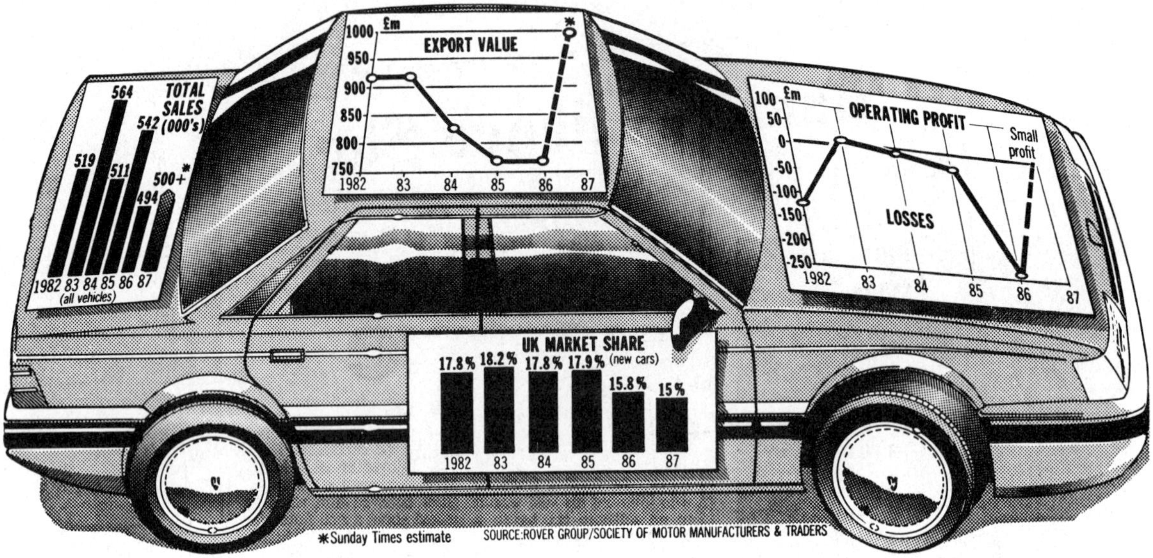

SOURCE: THE SUNDAY TIMES, 6 MARCH 1988

a British Airways recently bought out the Rover Group. What term could you use to describe this action?

b The Government had previously described the Rover Group as a 'lame duck'. In your own words, explain the meaning of this term. (Use the statistics to help you.)

c i) What has been the trend in the Rover Group's UK market share in recent years?
ii) Can you think of any reasons that would account for this trend?

d i) Who now owns the Rover Group?
ii) Who controls the Rover Group?
iii) How are the profits distributed?

e From the picture, what comments can you make on Rover's exports?

RETAIL OUTLETS

EXERCISE 37

Study the table below, which shows the distribution of retail outlets in Great Britain.

Retail outlets: regional distribution, 1984

	England		Scotland	
	Retail outlets (number)	Turnover (£ million)	Retail outlets (number)	Turnover (£ million)
Food retailers	91,884	27,109	8,770	2,764
Drink, confectionery and tobacco retailers	49,068	7,210	4,802	800
Clothing, footwear and leather goods retailers	48,831	6,400	3,954	641
Household goods retailers	49,919	10,447	3,838	913
Other non-food businesses	41,000	5,729	3,669	545
Mixed retail businesses	8,914	10,428	1,362	1,150
Hire and repair businesses	5,889	1,005	762	123
Total retail trade	295,505	68,327	27,158	6,936

	Wales		Great Britain	
	Retail outlets (number)	Turnover (£ million)	Retail outlets (number)	Turnover (£ million)
Food retailers	6,098	1,421	106,752	31,294
Drink, confectionery and tobacco retailers	2,937	382	56,808	8,391
Clothing, footwear and leather goods retailers	2,709	287	55,494	7,328
Household goods retailers	2,636	465	56,393	11,825
Other non-food businesses	1,865	234	46,533	6,508
Mixed retail businesses	600	492	10,876	12,069
Hire and repair businesses	253	35	6,904	1,163
Total retail trade	17,098	3,316	339,761	78,579

SOURCE: REGIONAL TRENDS, 1988

a i) What percentage of retail outlets in Great Britain are in England?
ii) Give TWO reasons which might account for this figure.

b What is the most common type of retail outlet in
i) England ii) Scotland iii) Wales?

c Explain in your own words what the item *turnover (£m)* means.

d There were over 17 000 retail outlets in Wales in 1984, a thousand fewer than in 1982 despite a 16 per cent increase in turnover. What might account for this trend?

e Make a list of any recent changes in the retailing business that could account for the increase in turnover.

SUPERSTORES AND HYPERMARKETS

EXERCISE 38

Examine the following tables.

Table 1: New Superstores & Hypermarkets

	Superstores (2,500–4,999 m²)		Hypermarkets (5,000 m²+)	
Year opened	Number opened in year	Cumulative total	Number opened in year	Cumulative total
1966	0	0	1	1
1967	1	1	1	2
1968	1	2	2	4
1969	6	8	0	4
1970	7	15	1	5
1971	4	19	0	5
1972	7	26	2	7
1973	11	37	1	8
1974	12	49	4	12
1975	9	58	3	15
1976	16	74	3	18
1977	19	93	3	21
1978	26	119	5	26
1979	19	138	3	29
1980	20	158	4	33
1981	28	186	2	35
1982	28	214	1	36
1983	22	236	0	36
1984	21	257	4	40
Planned	66	—	2	—

Table 2: Floorspace of Superstores & Hypermarkets

	Total (2,500 m²+)		
Retailer	Number open	Net floorspace '000 m²	Number planned
Asda	83	316	7
Carrefour	7	40	3
Co-operative Retail Services	11	31	1
Co-op (other societies)	32	121	4
Fine Fare	35	136	2
G T Smith & Sons	1	4	0
Gateway Foodmarkets	4	11	0
Hillards	5	15	3
International	3	9	0
Low, Wm.	1	3	0
Morrisons	14	42	1
Presto	5	15	1
Safeway	0	0	3
Sainsbury	14	39	24
SavaCentre	6	40	0
Stewarts	3	8	0
Tesco	61	236	14
Woolco	12	70	0
UK TOTAL	297	114	63

Table 3: Regional analysis of superstores 1985

Standard region	Number of stores	Total sales area '000 ft	Population '000 (1982)	'000 Population/ store
Scotland	42	1,548	5,167	123
Wales	29	1,038	2,808	97
North	23	1,049	3,107	135
Yorkshire and Humberside	48	1,670	4,910	102
North West	57	2,358	6,432	113
East Midlands	32	1,338	3,852	120
West Midlands	41	1,583	5,182	126
East Anglia	10	363	1,915	192
South East	88	3,459	17,005	193
South West	26	946	4,397	169
TOTAL	396	15,353	54,775	138

SOURCE: THE A TO Z OF UK RETAILING

a Using Table 1, plot two graphs:
i) cumulative total of superstores against year of opening;
ii) cumulative total of hypermarkets against year of opening.

b Using Table 2, draw a pie chart showing the percentage of the total number of hypermarkets and superstores owned by Asda, Carrefour, Co-operative Retail Services, Co-op (other societies), Fine Fare, Morrisons, Sainsbury, Tesco, Woolco and 'others'.

c According to the data, what is the difference between a superstore and a hypermarket?

d According to your graph, which type of store has shown the most rapid rate of growth over the years?

e For what reasons have these large stores been developed by the retailers?

f According to your pie chart, which company has the largest share of hypermarkets and superstores? Apart from floorspace and number of stores, what other measures of market share could be used?

g i) How is the *location* of a hypermarket likely to differ from that of a superstore?
ii) What are the advantages and disadvantages to the shopper of such a location?
iii) Why do proposals for hypermarkets cause planning problems for local councils, and why are they likely to be opposed by small traders and traders in town centres?

h Which retailer appeared to be planning the most rapid expansion of hypermarkets and superstores in 1985?

i i) Give two reasons for the falling number of sole traders engaged in retail grocery trade.
ii) In what ways can the sole trader compete with large stores?

THE MAIL ORDER MARKET

EXERCISE 39

Look carefully at the chart and graph.

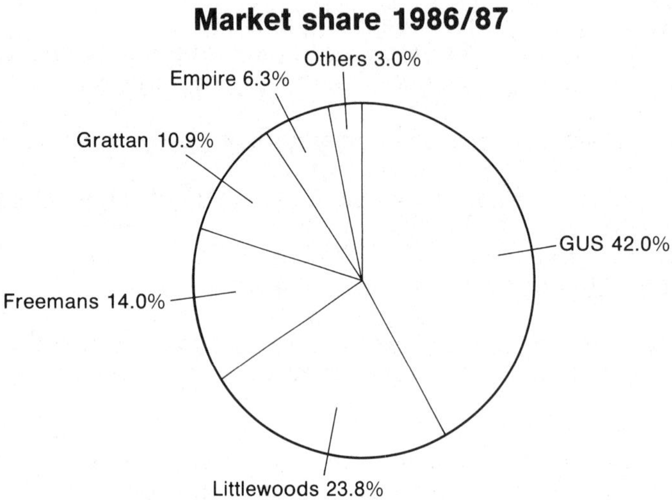

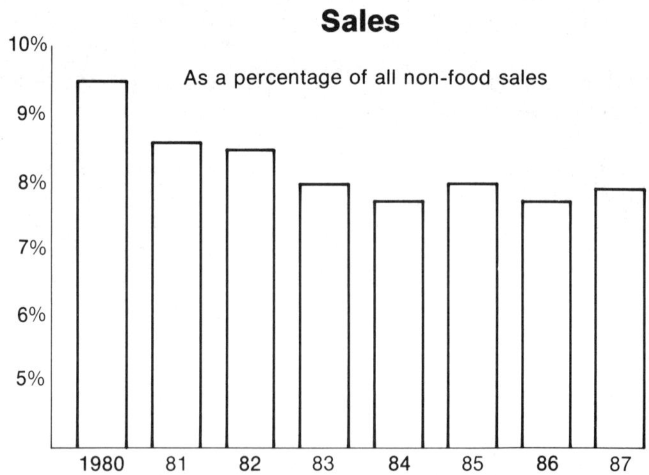

SOURCE: SUNDAY TELEGRAPH, 14 FEBRUARY 1988
(based on information from Verdict Research)

a Has Mail Order buying become more or less popular?

b What is the name of the Mail Order firm that had the greatest market share in 1986/87?

c What are the main problems faced by the Mail Order firms?

d Name TWO advantages of Mail Order shopping for the consumer.

THE WHOLESALER

EXERCISE 40

Study this diagram.

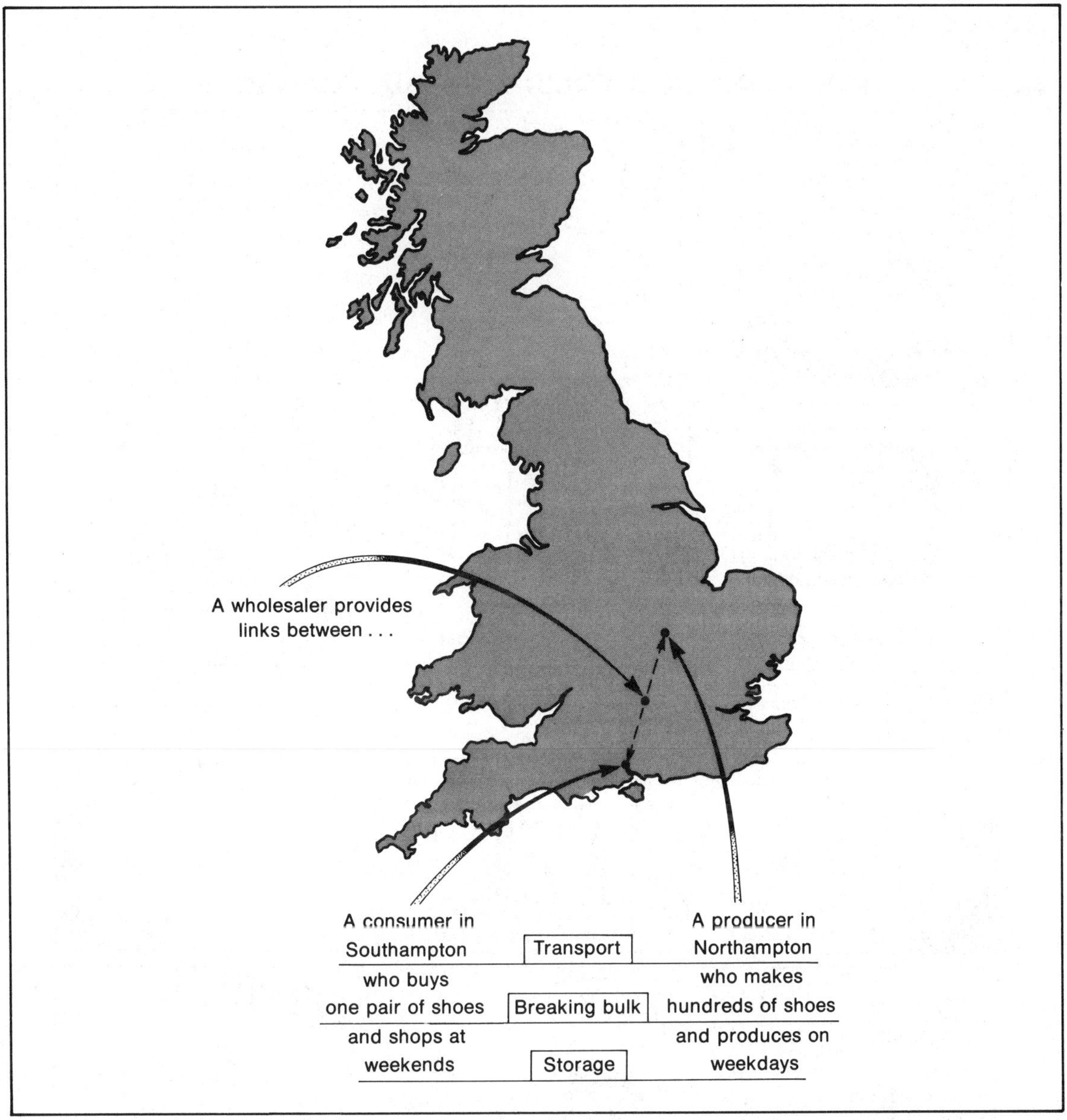

a Describe and explain the main functions of the wholesaler.

b It is sometimes said that the wholesaler transports goods through 'space' and 'time'. What is meant by this?

'LINKMAN' VOLUNTARY BUYING GROUPS

EXERCISE 41

Read the comic strip.

THE STORY OF A VOLUNTARY BUYING GROUP

a Mr Jones is in trouble because there are certain things which a large shop can do but he cannot. Make a list of these things, which are known as *Economies of Scale*.

b We all *know* that it is usually cheaper to 'buy in bulk', but we do not usually ask ourselves *why* this is so. Imagine that you are the producer of *Foamy Liquid*. Explain why you would prefer to sell one box of 1000 cartons of liquid to *Fairprice* rather than 100 boxes of 10 cartons to grocers like Mr Jones. Why is it worth your while reducing your price to *Fairprice*?

c i) Summarise the advantages to Mr Jones of belonging to the *Link* organisation.
ii) In what ways does *Link* earn its profits? What do you think happens to the profits of *Link*?

d Survey your town and neighbourhood, and you should find the name of several voluntary buying groups in the grocery trade (Spar and Nisa are two examples). See if you can also find the name of a voluntary buying group linking (i) newsagents, (ii) toyshops, and (iii) chemists. (*Note*: find out what is meant by a *franchise* and be sure not to confuse franchises with voluntary buying groups).

e When you have surveyed several voluntary buying group shops in the grocery trade, draw up a chart showing their location, opening hours, range of goods and typical prices. Insert on your chart similar information for two or three multiple chain stores (Tesco, Gateway, etc.) Comment on any patterns or trends that you find.

FREIGHT TRANSPORT

EXERCISE 42

Study the table below, which shows the different ways of transporting goods.

FREIGHT TRANSPORT BY MODE, 1976–1986			
Goods moved	percent (of tonne-km)		
	1976	1981	1986
Road	64	55	57
Rail	14	10	9
Water	18	29	28
of which:			
coastwise	15	25	20
internal	—	—	—
foreign	—	—	1
one-port	3	4	7
Pipeline	4	6	6
All modes	100	100	100

SOURCE: ECONOMIC TRENDS, 1988

a Construct a pie chart to show the percentage of goods moved by each mode of transport in 1986.

b i) The percentage of goods moved by rail has fallen in the last 10 years. What service has British Rail developed to improve the transport of goods?
ii) In your own words, briefly explain how this system works.

c Name ONE other mode of transport not mentioned in the table.

d Imagine you are the owner of a business that manufactures toys and exports a high proportion of them to European markets. What considerations would you need to take into account in deciding what method of transport to use?

PASSENGER TRANSPORT

EXERCISE 43

Study the following graph carefully, then answer the questions.

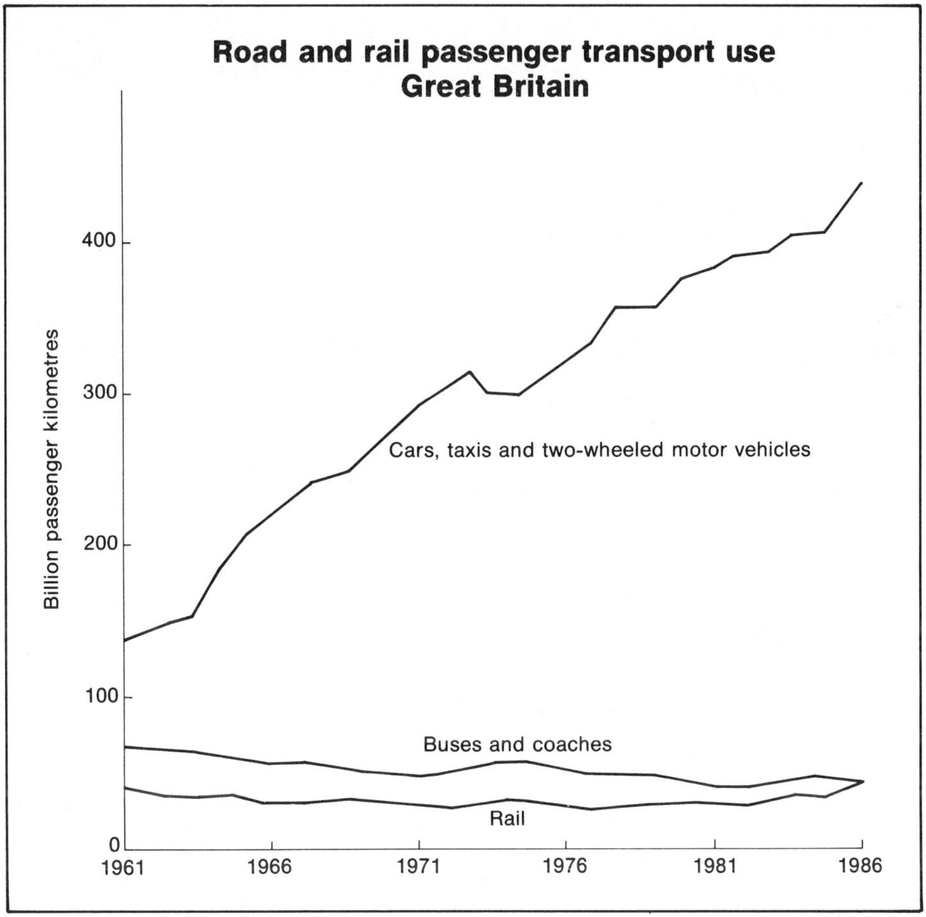

SOURCE: ECONOMIC TRENDS, 1988
(based on information from Department of Transport)

a What mode of passenger transport has increased most rapidly in the last 20 years?

b Comment on the use of rail transport over the last 20 years.

c What might account for road passenger transport being more popular than rail?

d Name TWO other modes of transport not referred to in the chart.

ROAD TRAFFIC

EXERCISE 44

Study the information about road traffic in different countries, then answer the questions that follow.

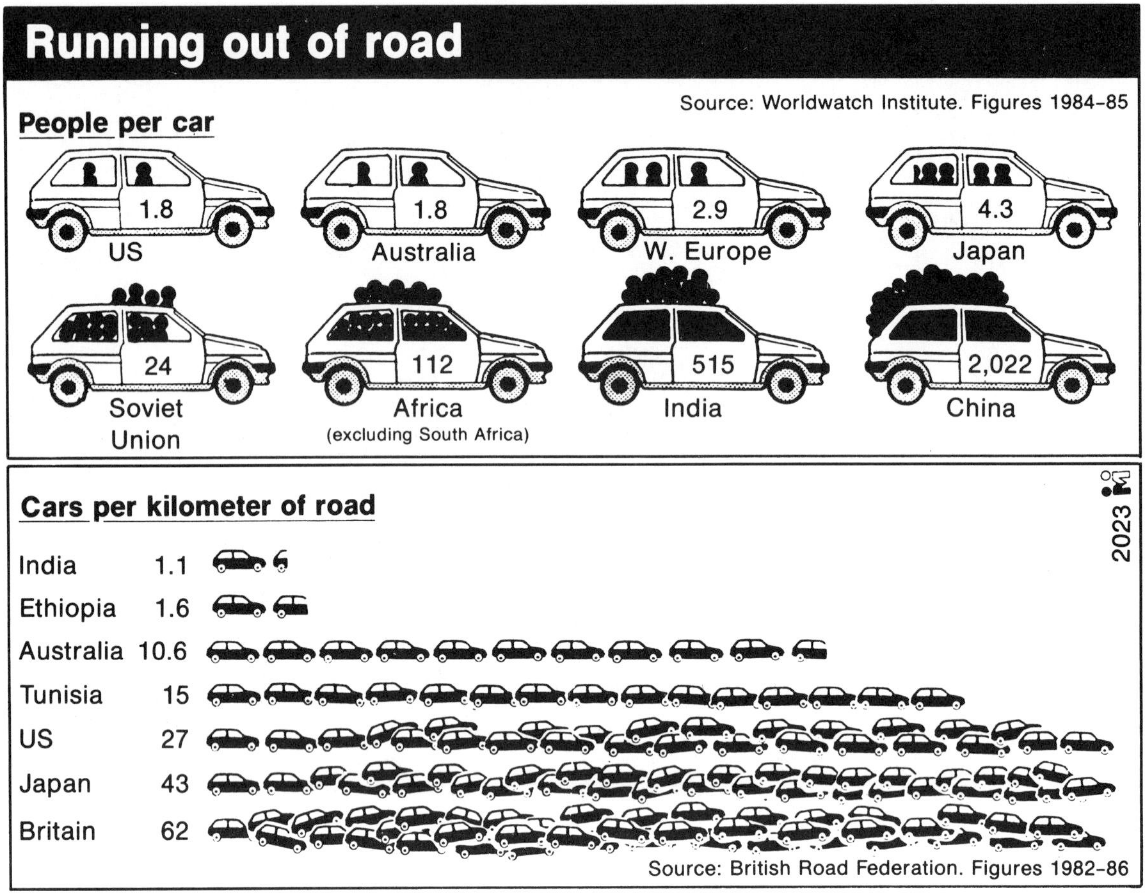

SOURCE: WESTERN MAIL, 13 SEPTEMBER 1988

a Suggest reasons for the low ratio of cars to population in China.

b Which country has:
   i) the least road traffic congestion?
   ii) the most road traffic congestion?

c Japan is one of the world's leading car producers.
   i) Why do you think Japan has more than twice as many people per car as Australia?
   ii) Why does Japan have four times as many cars per kilometre of road as Australia?

d What are the effects on a country of increasing road traffic congestion?

e Do the figures necessarily imply that there are fewer cars in India than in the USA?

AIR TRAVEL

EXERCISE 45

Study the following data carefully, then answer the questions.

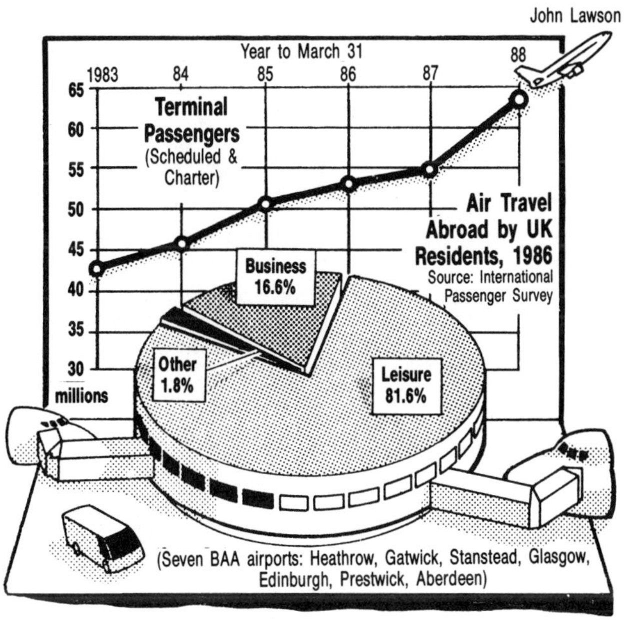

CARRYING ON

Airline	1987 Passengers
British Airways	19,435,779
British Airtours	2,690,401
British Caledonian	2,593,880
Britannia	6,218,295
Dan-Air	5,262,782
Monarch	2,419,150
Air Europe	1,638,553
Orion	1,602,399
British Midland	1,929,064
Others	8,218,966
Total	52,009,269

SOURCE: THE SUNDAY TIMES, 1 MAY 1988

a Draw a bar graph to show how many passengers travelled with each airline in 1987.

b Has the total number of passengers travelling abroad by air increased or decreased in recent years?

c For what purposes is air transport most commonly used?

d i) Suggest TWO reasons why air transport is preferred to sea travel.
ii) Are there any disadvantages with travelling by air?

e Why do you think that airline companies are able to offer 'cheap' flights abroad?

CONFLICT AT WORK

EXERCISE 46

Read these background details and scenario. You will then take part in a 'role-play' exercise.

THE PEOPLE IN CONFLICT

HAYLEY JONES
Aged 20, has been with the company for four years, since leaving school with five GCSEs. Currently being considered for promotion.

TRACY SMITH
Aged 18, joined the company six months ago after two years on a youth training scheme. Rather a shy girl, but generally regarded as a competent worker.

MIKE THOMAS
Aged 32, dynamic, keen, thought of as a militant by management. A production line worker.

C.J. TRUMAN
Aged 56, arrived in Britain from Canada at the age of 20 with the price of a bus ticket in his pocket. Now owns British Euroboxes, the largest manufacturer of card-board boxes in Western Europe. A self-made man.

JOYCE FERGUSON
Aged 40, a graduate of the Man-chester Business School. Has worked in senior positions in several companies.

STEVE WILLIAMS
Aged 20, studying sociology with the Open University in his spare time, would like to be a full-time union official. Has a clerical job at present. He has accused Mike Thomas in the past of 'poaching' members from his union.

GORDON HIGGINS
Aged 42, has worked his way up from the shop floor to become a supervisor after 27 years with the company. Recently applied for the job of personnel manager which was subsequently filled by Joyce Ferguson.

SCENARIO

Tracy Smith joined the company six months ago as a clerical assistant. Unfortunately, in recent weeks, a number of personal articles (including money) have gone missing.

Hayley Jones accuses Tracy of being a thief and insists that their supervisor should take the matter further. The supervisor, Gordon Higgins, agrees to do so. The personnel manager, Joyce Ferguson, is also informed of the matter and decides to hold a meeting where the following people will be present:

Hayley Jones (the accuser)
Mike Thomas (shop steward for SOGAT – Hayley's trade union)
Tracy Smith (the accused)
Steve Williams (shop steward for GMBTU – Tracy's trade union)
Gordon Higgins (supervisor)
Joyce Ferguson (personnel officer)

Joyce Ferguson will chair the meeting and asks in advance that Hayley and Tracy should each prepare a statement of their case. Gordon will also be asked to comment. Hayley and Tracy will each consult their respective shop stewards and attend the meeting with them.

a With the class split into groups of six, each of you will play one of the six characters. Joyce prepares an agenda for the meeting, the others prepare their statements and comments.

b Each group of six goes to a corner of the classroom to take part in the full meeting. Joyce takes minutes of the meeting.

c i) In a class session, your teacher will ask for the minutes to be read out by a representative of each group, and the class as a whole will discuss the proceedings and decisions taken, bearing in mind two questions:
1 Why do problems like this arise?
2 How are they best resolved?

ii) Write a summary of the findings of the class discussion.

d On the day of the meeting, the Chairman and Managing Director of the company, C.J. Truman, happens to be on the premises with Sid Harbottle, a journalist from *Woman's Herald*, who is writing a feature article about successful business people. 'C.J.' is furious when he finds out that Joyce has called this meeting and decides to tell her later that she should have handled the matter differently.

i) Write a memo from C.J. to Joyce stating why you are annoyed and outlining the alternative courses of action that could have been followed.

ii) Do *you* think C.J. is right to be annoyed? Justify your answer.

e Read again carefully the background details, and your answer to task (c), and look for sources of potential conflict (reasons why these people might be expected to clash sooner or later). There are several possible reasons, not only in the personalities and backgrounds of the characters, but also in their view of their responsibilities within the firm (for instance: need Joyce have been informed about this matter? Who should decide whether or not to tell her? Would C.J. normally be interested?)

Write a paragraph identifying as many possible sources of conflict as you can.

PAY PATTERNS

Study the following tables carefully and then answer the questions.

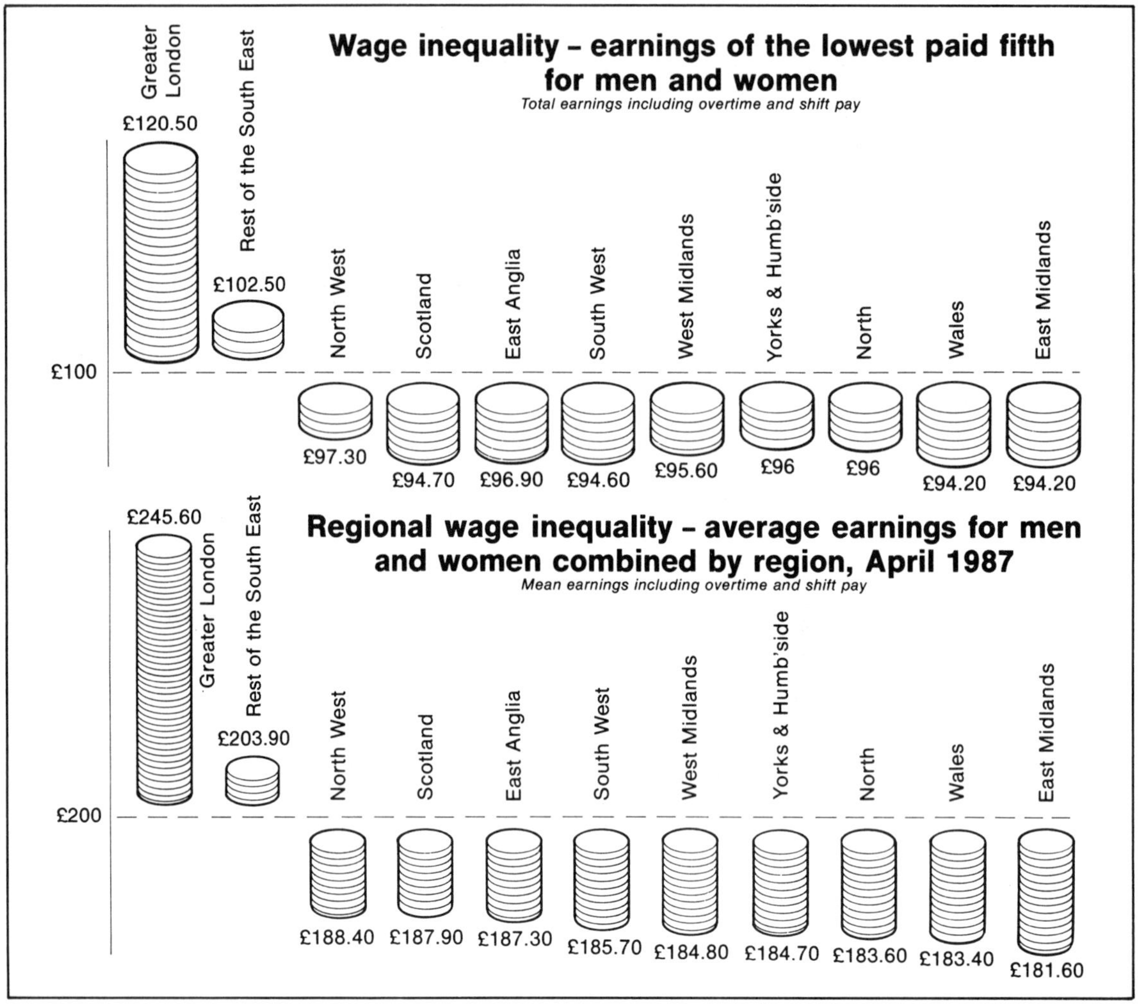

SOURCE: WESTERN MAIL, 28 APRIL 1988
(from Department of Employment, New Earnings Survey, 1987, HMSO)

a What are the average earnings for men and women in the South East of England, excluding Greater London?

b Which region has the lowest average earnings?

c The figures for average earnings include *overtime* and *shift pay*. What do these terms mean?

d Make a list of reasons why average earnings are so much higher in Greater London compared to the East Midlands.

SALARY LEVELS

EXERCISE 48

Study the data carefully then answer the questions.

SKILLED STAFF

SALARY LEVELS

Whilst Personal Disposable Incomes are rising fast in Wales, salary levels for professional staff are still well below the UK average.

Average weekly earnings, non manual workers, by industry, April 1986 selected industry groups (£ per week).

	Wales		South East		UK	
	Male	Female	Male	Female	Male	Female
Banking, Finance Insurance etc	223.8	120.0	306.5	170.8	271.2	148.5
Professional and Scientific Services	241.6	156.0	250.6	172.2	242.6	165.8
All Non-Manufacturing Industries	218.8	134.5	265.5	161.6	241.2	145.0

SOURCE: WESTERN MAIL, 29 MARCH 1988

a What is the average weekly wage of women in the Professional and Scientific Services in Wales?

b i) What are the average weekly earnings of men in the Banking, Finance, Insurance sector for the UK?
ii) Give ONE reason why the figure for women in the same sector is so much lower.

c The Equal Pay Act was passed in 1976. What was the purpose of this act?

d 'Personal disposable incomes are rising fast in Wales.' What does the term 'personal disposable income' mean?

e Give reasons why personal disposable incomes in the South East are above the national average.

WORKING HOURS

EXERCISE 49

Study the two charts carefully, then answer the questions that follow.

Weekly hours of work and paid holidays: full-time manual employees United Kingdom

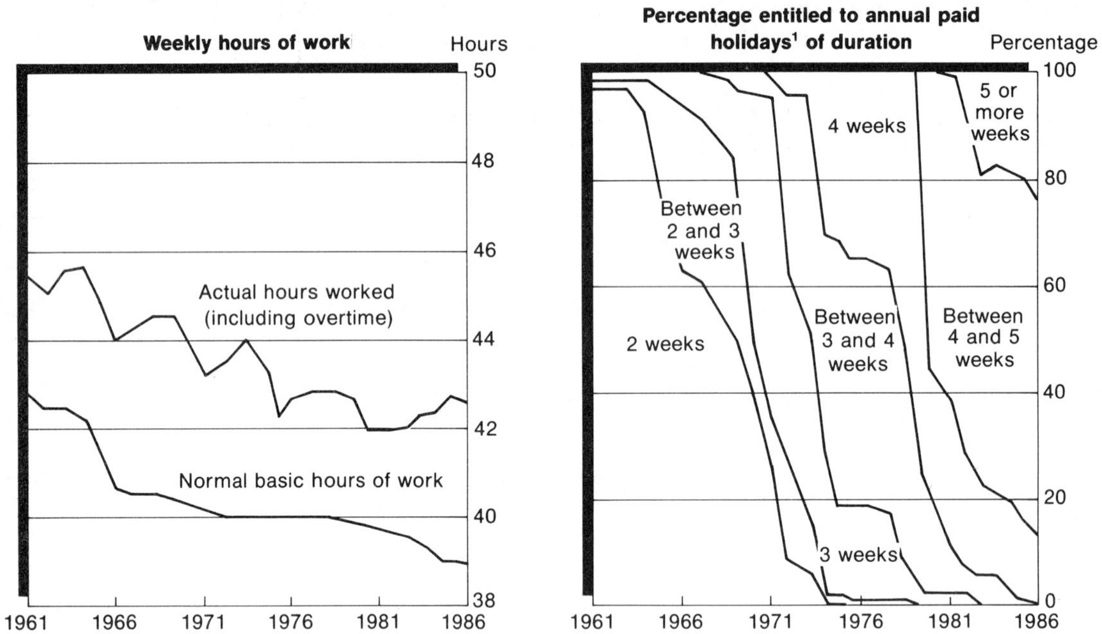

[1]The information relates to basic entitlements in national collective agreements or Wages Council Orders.

SOURCE: SOCIAL TRENDS, 1988
(based on information from Department of Employment)

a Compare the basic number of hours worked in 1976 and 1986.

b Apart from overtime, why do you think the actual hours worked in a week are greater than the basic hours worked?

c Non manual employees are often referred to as 'white collar' workers. What are manual workers called?

d What percentage of people in 1986 were entitled to more than five weeks paid holiday a year?

e i) Has the number of paid holidays increased or decreased in the last 10 years?
ii) Give TWO reasons to support your answer.

JOB ADVERTISEMENT

EXERCISE 50

Study this fictitious job advertisement carefully.

> **THE *PIZZA PLACE* PLC**
>
> Are you bright, out-going, enthusiastic, and not afraid of hard work?
>
> The *Pizza Place* chain of restaurants requires
>
> **TRAINEE MANAGERS**
>
> Salaries start at £8060 p.a. in training, rising to £12000 for Assistant Managers, and can reach £17000 for Senior Managers plus profits bonus of up to £10000.
>
> Write for application form or send your c.v. to:
>
> Anita Khan,
> Personnel Unit,
> Pizza Place PLC,
> London, WC99 9ZZ

a The *Pizza Place* is part of the service sector. Why are the opportunities for employment in this type of industry likely to increase in the future?

b The salaries advertised start at £8060. What deductions are likely to be made from these figures?

c i) What is a *Curriculum Vitae* or *CV*?
ii) Draw up a CV for yourself, including relevant details.
iii) Write a letter of application for this post to accompany your CV.

d Suppose you were called for an interview for this post.
i) What questions might you be asked?
ii) What questions would you wish to ask?

e Explain the meaning of the following terms which are often used in connection with job advertisements and applications:
i) fringe benefits
ii) an equal opportunities employer
iii) bonus schemes
iv) flexitime
v) job sharing
vi) leave entitlement
vii) shortlist
viii) weighting allowance
ix) non-contributory pension scheme
x) relocation expenses

INDUSTRIAL RELATIONS

EXERCISE 51

Study this information.

Industrial disputes - working days lost and number of stoppages (UK)

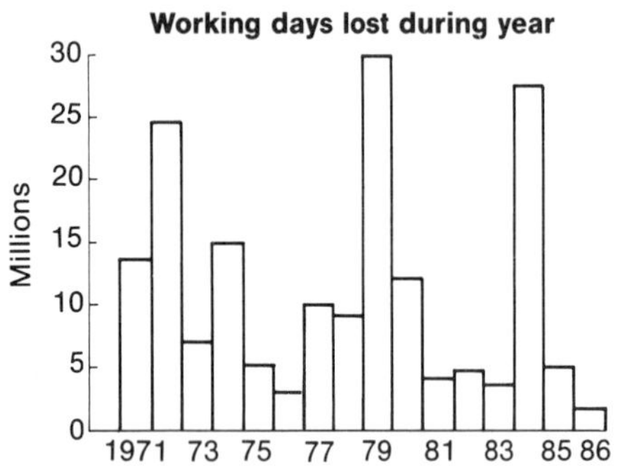

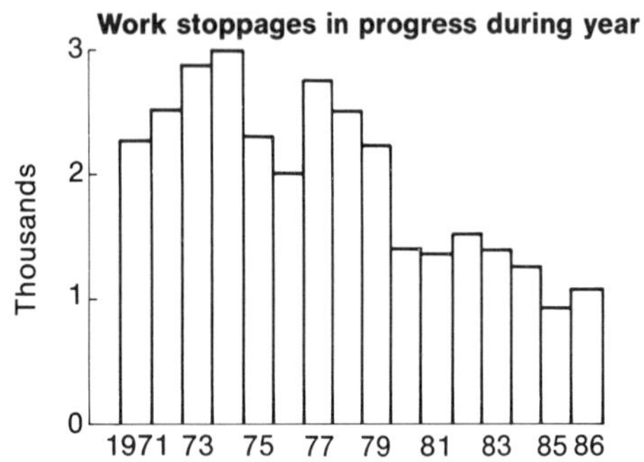

There were 1.9 million working days lost through stoppages of work during 1986 in the United Kingdom, the lowest total since 1963 when 1.8 million working days were lost. This compares with 6.4 million in 1985 and an annual average of 11.1 million for the ten years 1976 to 1985. The largest dispute in 1986 in terms of working days lost was the nationwide strike by teachers accounting for 13 per cent (0.3 million working days) of the total. The relatively high numbers of working days lost during 1984 (27.1 million) was largely due to the miners' strike which accounted for 83 per cent of the total. A total of 26.3 million working days were lost during this dispute, which began in March 1984 and ended in March 1985.

The number of stoppages recorded as being in progress in 1986 was 1,074, compared to 903 in 1985, 1,221 in 1984 and an annual average of 1,693 over the ten years 1976 to 1985. The total for 1986 was the second lowest recorded for any year since 1940, when 925 stoppages were recorded. However, comparisons over time must be made with caution due to the difficulties in ensuring complete recording. It is partly for this reason, and partly because they are a better measure of the impact of disputes, that the figures for working days lost are regarded as a better indicator of the effects of stoppages of work due to industrial disputes. The *Trade Union Act 1984* made a strike unlawful without a ballot paper which makes it clear that the workers were being asked whether they were prepared to act in breach of their contracts of employment.

SOURCE: SOCIAL TRENDS, 1988

a Explain the difference between an 'official' and an 'unofficial' dispute.

b Describe the problems of measuring the effects of industrial disputes.

c Less than half of the working population of the UK belongs to a trade union. Although this is quite a high proportion compared with many other countries, membership of British trade unions at the end of 1988 was approximately 9 million, a fall of 3 million over a five year period. Industrial unions are losing members, while 'white collar' unions are expanding, and several unions have merged or are considering mergers. Suggest possible reasons for these trends.

d Follow the news regarding Trade Unions for a few weeks, and keep a diary of the main events. Keep an eye open especially for any mention of the following:

i) single-union agreements
ii) no-strike deals
iii) pendulum arbitration
iv) the role of the TUC

Discuss these items in class with your teacher, then write a paragraph explaining why they are important issues.

e Trade Unions do not exist in order to organise disputes. Make a list of reasons for joining a Trade Union.

COMMUNICATIONS

EXERCISE 52

Look at this label.

Datapost

A Royal Mail Service

EMS Datapost

Order number

Date sent

Contract number

To

Press Hard You are making six copies
Please type or press firmly with a ballpoint pen

18686759

D P 1 8 6 8 6 7 5 9 G B

Total items in consignment

This item

No. of

Enter YES if Saturday delivery required

From

EMS Datapost

1. Finance copy — period of retention 2 years

SOURCE: THE POST OFFICE

a Datapost guarantees overnight delivery of packages. What other services does the Post Office provide for businesses that wish to communicate?

b Describe how telecommunications and electronic mail provide an alternative to paper communications. Do you think that telecommunications will eventually replace mail completely? Give reasons for your answer.

THE WORKING POPULATION

EXERCISE 53

Look carefully at this graph. The *activity rate* or *participation rate* is the ratio of the working population to the total population.

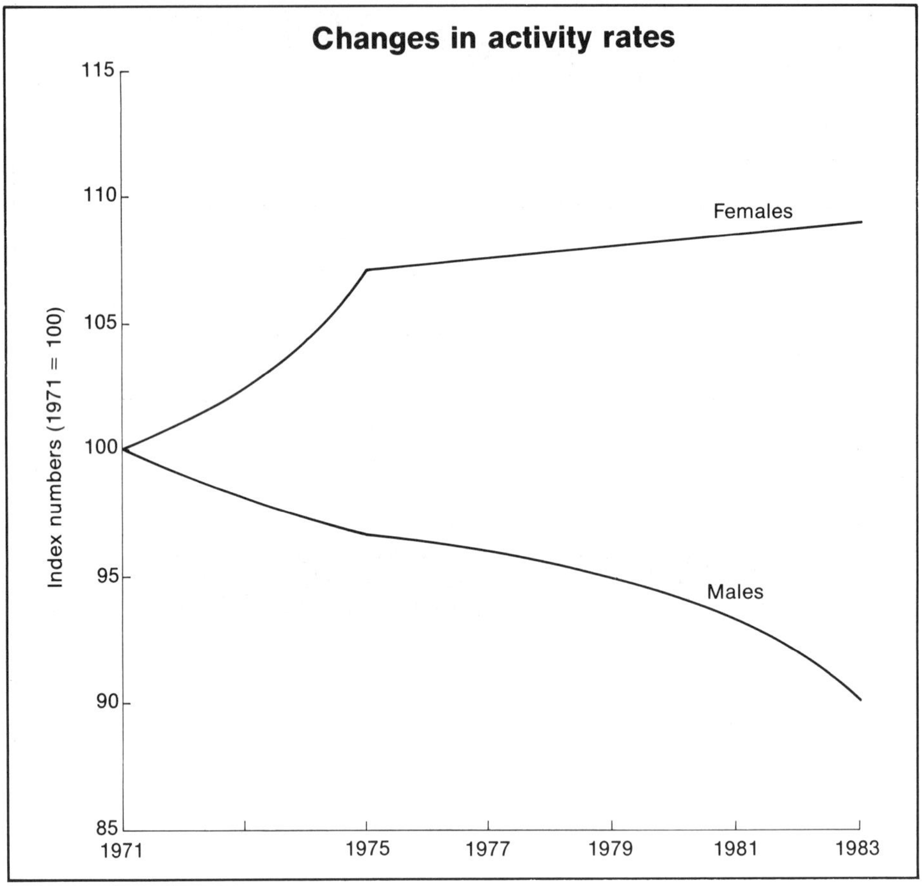

SOURCE: ECONOMIC TRENDS, 1988

a What has happened to the activity rates of men and women over this period of time?

b The graph does NOT show us how the *size* of the working population has changed. It tells us something about the *composition* of the working population. How far do you think activity rates have been affected by the following trends?

i) New attitudes towards women going out to work.
ii) Declining birth rates and smaller families.
iii) Closure of industries which traditionally employed males, together with earlier retirement.
iv) Foreign investment in Britain in assembly-line factories which employ large numbers of women.
v) Easy credit financing a retail boom which encourages imported consumer durables to be sold at the expense of home-produced goods.
vi) The expansion of service industries and part-time employment.

c How might the changes in activity rates be expected to affect
i) the wage costs of businesses
ii) family life
iii) trade unions
iv) government policy?

d Think about whether the increased activity rates are 'good news' for women's opportunities. Are the jobs being taken up by women as well paid as those lost by males? Is it true that shop workers tend to be women, while shop managers tend to be men? (Can you think of workplaces where the opposite is true?) Are more women pursuing 'careers' through choice, or taking on 'jobs' through economic necessity? Write a report summarising your conclusions.

KNOW YOUR RIGHTS

EXERCISE 54

Read this comic strip.

A DAY IN THE LIFE OF TOMMY TROUBLE

7.30 a.m. While pouring out his cornflakes, Tommy discovers a dead beetle in the packet.

10.00 a.m. At work, Tommy slips on a pool of fluid from a machine that is leaking. Management had been informed of the leak at 9.15 a.m. In anger, he swears at the foreman and is instantly dismissed for 'gross misconduct'.

11.30 a.m. Tommy decides to return the new suit he bought yesterday from a town centre shop. He asks for his money back because he says he has changed his mind about the colour. The suit is still in perfect condition.

12.30 p.m. He returns to his car at a Council car park, to find that it has been severely scraped. On the wall, the following sign is clearly displayed: 'THE COUNCIL ACCEPTS NO RESPONSIBILITY FOR DAMAGE TO VEHICLES, HOWEVER CAUSED.' Tommy has no evidence of the cause of the damage.

1.30 p.m. Tommy catches a taxi home. The fare is £3. He offers the driver £3 in 2p pieces. He has a £5 note in his pocket.

4.30 p.m. A double-glazing representative calls at Tommy's home. To get rid of the rep., he agrees to buy some panes on hire purchase, believing that he will be allowed to change his mind.

a Tommy has certain legal rights as an employee and as a consumer. For each of the six situations shown:

i) Write a note to Tommy telling him what his rights are.

ii) Where relevant, name a piece of legislation which covers the circumstances shown.

b In those situations where you think the law is on Tommy's side, include in your note to Tommy an outline of the steps he could take to obtain his rights.

INSURANCE · 1 ·

EXERCISE 55

Study this information.

A WAGE FOR LIFE

SULTRY singer Sabrina, right, reckons her boobs are her biggest asset, so she's insured them for £100,000 each.

If you fear that injury or illness may cut short your career then Permanent Health Insurance will guarantee you a set income up to retirement if need be.

A man of 30 wanting £150 a week after being off work for three months would have to pay £2 to £4 a week depending on what he does. Dangerous jobs, cost more, or might not get cover at all.

SOURCE: DAILY MIRROR, 4 JANUARY 1989

LLOYDSAMONEY!

Lloyd's is not a company, but a market which has taken on almost every kind of risk from deep-space satellites to deep-sea cables, with aircraft, oil tankers, earthquakes and hurricanes along the way.

Some Lloyd's insurance policies look decidedly eccentric. Underwriters there have insured whisky-tasters' palates, the actress Betty Grable's legs (for a million dollars the pair) and an American elephant on water-skis. Cutty Sark whisky once offered a million-pound prize to anyone who could find the Loch Ness monster – but insured themselves at Lloyd's against the risk of coming up with a winner.

SOURCE: ADAPTED FROM THE OBSERVER MAGAZINE, 31 JULY 1988

a i) Name the three principles of insurance.
ii) Explain how the unusual insurance policies mentioned in the extracts satisfy the three principles.

b 'Lloyd's is not a company, but a market.' What does this phrase mean?

c Describe the work of an underwriter.

d Unlike the other insurance policies mentioned, Permanent Health Insurance is not at all 'unusual'. Apart from Permanent Health Insurance, what types of insurance policy are likely to be held by an average family?

e Explain how (i) actuaries and (ii) assessors help to make insurance a profitable business.

INSURANCE ·2·

Study this leaflet.

BUSINESS INSURANCE

The obvious reasons for insuring your business – fire, theft and so on – are not the only questions you'll need to consider. What if fire in a neighbouring property forces you to close down for a time? What would happen to your business should a partner or fellow director unexpectedly become ill or even die? And if you employ people, there are legal insurance obligations as well.

We offer advice and cover on most aspects of business life.

LLOYDS BANK BUSINESS INSURANCE

We can offer cover to meet most eventualities – such as loss or damage to property or contents through fire, flood or theft; business interruption and loss of profits; public and employers' liability. Special policies are available for particular types of business. We would be glad to advise and quote on your special needs.

RETAILERS' PROTECTION PROGRAMME

The most extensive policy of its kind, covering every aspect of business; specifically designed for retailers, restaurateurs and publicans.

PENSIONS

This can prove a cost-effective and tax-efficient method of providing for your own retirement – and rewarding those who help you build a business. We will be very pleased to help you find the pension plan most appropriate for your needs.

KEYPERSON INSURANCE

Provides security against the death or incapacity of a director, partner, or employee with special skills.

TO ENSURE SUCCESSION

Policies that provide funds for buying the shares of a retiring or deceased business partner or director, and so ensure that the business can continue without financial problems.

SOURCE: LLOYDS BANK SMALL BUSINESS SERVICES

a Make a list of as many different types of insurance policies as you can which might be held by both individual persons *and* businesses.

b What types of insurance are of interest mainly to businesses?

c Suppose you were the owner of a corner shop. What types of business insurance would you want?

Read the article and study the diagram.

Hi-tech store for Harrods

● A £25m computerised warehouse will cut costs and speed up deliveries

HARRODS is "moving into the 21st century". In a £25m modernisation programme the "top people's" store is installing the latest techniques for ordering, controlling and delivering the 5m different products it sells.

It has built a huge "high-bay" warehouse in which they will be stored to a computer's order. Each sales-point in the Knightsbridge store will be connected directly with the stock-control computer to speed up, and cut the cost of, deliveries to customers.

The warehouse is at Osterley, west London — seven miles or a 30-minute van-drive from the store — to replace an antiquated Victorian building in Barnes, further out.

The new warehouse is the biggest in Britain, the second largest in Europe and will handle a larger range of items than any other single distribution centre in the world. It is 442ft long, 427ft wide and 69ft high — more voluminous than a jumbo-jet hangar.

But what will really distinguish it is the use of computers on an extent not seen before in this industry. They will control or monitor every facet of warehouse, from loading, packing and dispatch to energy consumption.

Goods coming into the warehouse are given a bar-code by the computer that matches the "address" of a location in the racks. When the goods are loaded on to a Maestro, an on-board computer tells the driver where to take them. The operator carries a laser reader to check that the item's bar-code matches the one on the shelf where he is placing the goods.

For the first time, Harrods' managers will know, down to the last item, what stock they hold and where it is.

When a customer in the Knightsbridge store orders an item, the salesperson will look up its availability on a computer screen, decide with the buyer a delivery date and time, and instantly file the order to the warehouse. There a human operator sets off again on the Maestro, locates the goods and takes them to the packaging department for delivery.

The warehouse will improve service to the customer and cut costs. The aim, says Sandy Glenn, the store's director of distribution, is to cut by half the waiting period for an order, typically now a week for a three-piece suite, and to guarantee time of delivery to the customer "to within an hour".

Amit Roy

SOURCE: THE SUNDAY TIMES, 12 JUNE 1988

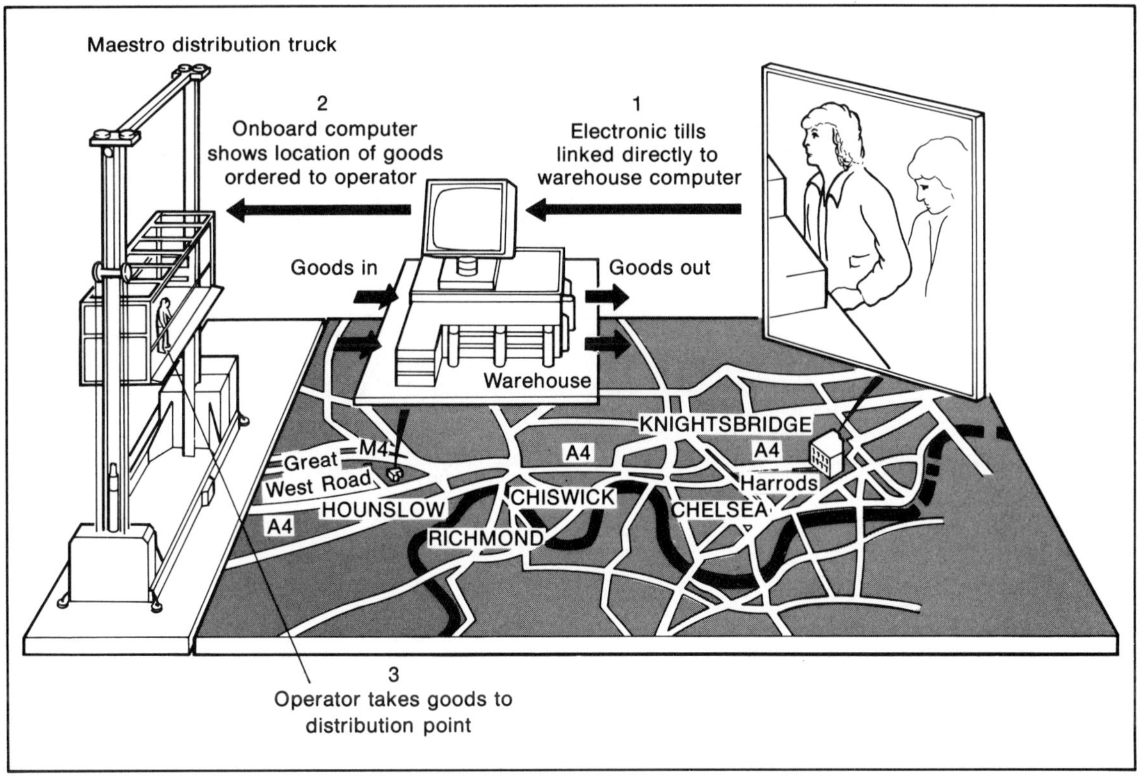

SOURCE: ADAPTED FROM THE SUNDAY TIMES, 12 JUNE 1988

a What is the purpose of a large warehouse to a store like Harrods?

b Warehousing was one function previously performed by the wholesaler. Why do large superstores no longer need this service?

c Study the system shown in the diagram and suggest any advantages to Harrods of adopting this system.

d What is the main problem of using this system?

e In your own words, explain how a computerised warehouse works.

Read this article.

Electronic pricing 'fleecing shoppers'

By ROGER DOBSON, Social Affairs Correspondent

SUPERMARKET customers are facing instant price increases.

Customers are having to pay price increases before they even hand over the cash for what they picked off the shelves, according to a new report.

New computer-based pricing systems mean that prices can be increased instantaneously at the touch of a button.

And in some cases customers are getting hit by the price increases before they even get to the checkout according to the report.

Today, in a new report, consumer chiefs have called for new controls over the use of the bar codes by supermarkets.

The consumer officers of local councils are now keeping a close eye on the new electronic systems after a series of complaints from shoppers.

Some want it made illegal for shops to increase the price of goods during the hours they are open, according to the report.

Others want complaint books to be kept at checkouts to record the comments of customers.

And there is concern that many of the mistakes may not be picked up by customers when direct debiting of bank accounts is brought in at supermarket checkouts.

Under the bar code system, instead of putting price labels on individual goods, stores put the price on the shelf and put the code on each item. The code is then read by a scanner at the checkout.

The report says, "Guidelines say that price increases should not be applied during trading hours.

"Yet a major source of error is price changes which take place during shopping hours. So perhaps it should be made illegal to increase prices during normal trading hours."

The report, from the National Consumer Council, says, "Customers are facing over-charging on store bar codes."

It says that guidelines on the use of the bar codes — including a ban on price increases during shopping hours — does [sic] exist but that most stores disregard it.

"The guidelines call for strict control to ensure the shelf ticket is showing the correct price before the computer file price is changed," says the report.

It adds, "Our experience shows that most stores appear to be disregarding these guidelines. There is no doubt that consumer confidence has been shaken."

The report says that if customers are overcharged both the company and the shop manager could be prosecuted. It says fines of up to £2,000 are possible.

The report says, "Trading standards officers are keeping a watchful eye on the systems and perhaps the guidelines should now require a complaints book to be kept at checkouts to log details of any pricing problems.

"What is needed is a real commitment from companies today to follow the guidelines and wipe out the doubts from consumers' minds."

It adds, "With the next step the direct debiting of the checkout bill from the customer's bank account, customer confidence in the system takes on enormous significance."

Store manager inputs new prices . . . Housewife chooses bargain beans at old price 36p . . .

. . . Laser scans new bar code price 39p . . . At home a housewife discovers too late

SOURCE: WESTERN MAIL, 6 JANUARY 1989

a What is a *bar code*?

b What are the advantages of bar codes
i) for shoppers
ii) for shopkeepers?

c Why is it important that shoppers should have confidence in the bar code system?

d Explain what would be involved in the 'direct debiting of the checkout bill', and why it is even more important that shoppers should have confidence in this system.

e If you got home with your groceries to find that the bar code system had charged you higher prices than you had expected, what steps could you take to put matters right?

ADVERTISING STANDARDS

EXERCISE 59

This illustration shows an advertisement placed in a newspaper by the Advertising Standards Authority (ASA). This body is concerned with advertisements which are misleading or offend against the British Code of Advertising Practice. This is a voluntary code adopted by the advertising industry, which finances the ASA.

SOURCE: ASA

Now consider the following fictitious advertisements, which might appear in newspapers or magazines or on hoardings.

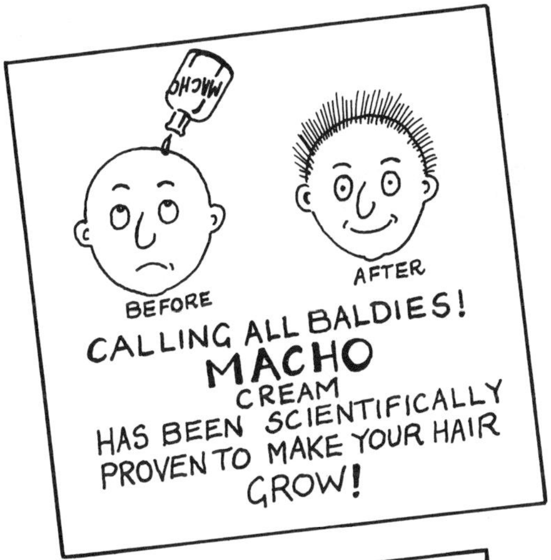

a Take each advertisement in turn and state in which ways, if any, they are illegal, indecent, dishonest or untruthful.

b Choose one of the fictitious advertisements and write a letter to the ASA giving reasons why you think it should be withdrawn.

c Now consider the ASA's own advertisement. How helpful is it to anyone who wishes to complain about an advertisement? Apart from the address of the ASA, what other information would be useful to someone thinking of making a complaint?

d Obtain a copy of the British Code of Advertising Practice, and details of how the ASA is organised and financed. The ASA has been described as having 'no teeth'. Write a paragraph to say whether you agree or disagree.

MAIL ORDER PROTECTION

EXERCISE 60

Read this paragraph concerning the Mail Order Protection Scheme (MOPS) which has been set up by the Newspaper Publishers' Association (NPA).

Shopping by post?

Play it safe

Readers who reply to cash with order advertisements in national newspapers or colour supplements are safeguarded by the National Newspapers Mail Order Protection Scheme. This covers all categories of goods and services with the exception of: those advertised under classified headings, perishable foodstuffs, horoscopes, lucky charms, non durable gardening and medical products.

The MOPS protection guarantees that your money will be refunded if a member advertiser stops trading and does not deliver your order, or refund your payment.

Advertisements covered by the Scheme may include the MOPS symbol or the initial letters MOPS in their layout.

For full details send a 9″ × 6″ stamped addressed envelope to:
The National Newspapers' Mail Order,
Protection Scheme,
16 Tooks Court, London, EC4A 1LB

Play it safe—look for the symbol

THE NATIONAL NEWSPAPER

MOPS

MAIL ORDER PROTECTION SCHEME

Readers' Protection Scheme Mail Order Advertising

With effect from April 1, 1975, national newspapers have set up a Central Fund to refund monies sent by readers in response to mail order advertisements placed by mail order traders who fail to supply goods or refund the money and who have become the subject of liquidation or bankruptcy proceedings. This arrangement does not apply to any failure to supply goods advertised in a catalogue or direct mail solicitation. These refunds are made on a voluntary basis on behalf of the contributors of the Fund and the readers' claims are limited to the Newspaper Publishers' Association on behalf of the contributors.

(a) Mail Order Advertising is defined as direct response advertisements, display or postal bargains, where cash has to be sent in advance of goods being received. Classified advertising and gardening features are excluded.

(b) Classified advertising is defined as advertising that appears under a "Classification" heading (excluding "Postal and Weekend Shopping") or within the classified columns or sections.

For the purpose of the Scheme.

In the unhappy event of the failure of a mail order trader, readers are advised to lodge a claim with the newspapers concerned within three months from the date of appearance of the advertisement. Any claim received after this period may be considered at the discretion of the NPA.

The establishment of this Fund enables you to respond to these advertisements with confidence.

SOURCE: MOPS

a The MOPS scheme is, in effect, a kind of insurance. What is the *risk* that the NPA is trying to insure readers against?

b Explain the meaning of the terms *liquidation* and *bankruptcy* (line 5).

c How do the *mail order* traders mentioned in line 3 differ from the *catalogue* traders and *direct mail solicitation* mentioned in lines 7 and 8?

d i) Distinguish between *mail order* and *classified advertising* as defined by the NPA (lines 12–15).

ii) Why do you think *classified* advertising is excluded from the MOPS scheme (lines 15–16)?

e Give two advantages and two disadvantages of purchasing goods from a newspaper by mail order.

f Look at the Saturday or Sunday edition of a popular newspaper. Make a list of the main types of goods that are offered through mail order. Comment on your findings.

ENTERPRISE AGENCIES

EXERCISE 61

Study this extract.

> SIXTEEN local enterprise agencies will be able to provide business advice to entrepreneurs more quickly and efficiently after a special computer link with two databases.
>
> The databases, developed at Strathclyde University, are managed by EPRC, one of the university's associated companies, and cover sources of government assistance for British business as well as the regulations with which British business must comply.
>
> Peter Quine, directing the project on behalf of the agencies for Business in the Community, said the venture would substantially enhance the ability of agencies to meet the needs of business.
>
> The 16 agencies are at: Blackburn, Bolton, Bristol New Work Trust, Cambridge, Doncaster, Milton Keynes, Newcastle (Project North East and Entrust), Plymouth, Runcorn, St Helens, Sheffield, Shropshire, Glasgow, Deeside, Merthyr Tydfil, Ogwr.

SOURCE: THE GUARDIAN, 3 JANUARY 1989

a What is a *database*? Explain why they are important to businesses.

b Enterprise Agencies have been set up in many localities, sponsored by local authorities, industry and banks. They provide premises, finance and advice to small businesses.

i) From *Yellow Pages* or your library, find out the name and address of your nearest Enterprise Agency.

ii) Write to or visit the Agency, and obtain information on the services it provides. Many agencies have an Educational Liaison Officer who will be pleased to speak to you.

iii) Suppose you wished to set yourself up in business as a mobile hairdresser. Make a list of what you would need to get started, and of the ways in which your local Enterprise Agency would help.

Read this newspaper article carefully.

Hey, big spenders — it looks like the party's over

Mark Milner and Daniel John

THE PARTY'S OVER. That's official. We have all been having too much fun nipping down the high street — plastic waving — and overspending which has pushed the balance of payments heavily into the red.

Now we are going to have to pay for all that profligacy. The Chancellor, Mr Nigel Lawson, has decreed: "You can have too much of a good thing. The economy is growing too fast. It is necessary to apply the brakes and that is what I have done."

In this case the brakes are cast in the form of higher bank base rates which will inevitably force a rise in the cost of home loans.

The idea runs like this. If you want to make sure people spend less, you make sure they have less to spend. Raising taxes is out — after all they were only cut in the last budget — while credit controls are scarcely welcome in the Thatcherite free market.

At least on the face of it, engineering an increase in mortgage rates is a pretty nifty alternative. It catches an awful lot of people and it hits their regular spending patterns.

Building Society Association (BSA) figures for the end of 1987 suggest that for every one per cent rise in the mortgage rate, home buyers have to shell out another £2 billion a year in extra interest payments. On that basis the mortgage increase we have already had, coupled with a 1.25 per cent rise in October, would have the effect of soaking up about £6 billion that might otherwise have gone on such economic undesirables as (imported) televisions, videos, and 'F' registered cars.

However, given the buoyancy of mortgage lending and house prices that figure is likely to be somewhat higher.

The BSA reckons that a rise of one per cent in home loan equals 0.67 per cent of personal disposable income. If that looks small beer just remember that the worrying trade deficit this year — even on worst case predictions — is likely to total about £13 billion. So the mortgage increase has the potential to make a big enough dent in spending to make the Chancellor smile again.

But for most of us, less concerned with the overall economic impact of our spending decisions, the mortgage increases will also make a tidy hole in our surplus disposable income.

Assuming another 1.25 per cent rise, anyone with a £30,000 repayment mortgage will be paying £45.60 a month more than last month. On a £60,000 mortgage, payments will rise by about £110 to just over £600 a month. But it is not only consumers who will suffer. The rise is also bad news for retailers who, until now, have ridden high on a "spend, spend and spend even more" mentality.

Retail spending is at about £170 billion a year and high street stores had been banking on growth of 3.4 per cent next year. But it now seems certain it will be less than 3 per cent. Another rise in base rates will eat into that even further, sending retailers into a spin.

And they now find themselves heading into a trap shaped largely by the consumer boom out of which stores have done so well.

As demand has increased, the big chains have been opening more outlets. But this needs greater investment which inevitably is money borrowed from the banks.

The stores also have to pay more for this space. The explosion in property values in the past five years has sent rent and rates soaring while wages for staff continue to rise by an average 8 per cent a year.

More money, not less, then has to find its way into the tills if this expansion is to be paid for. But all the current signs point to the lower level. That much was summed up in one simple phrase by a City analyst yesterday. "All the costs are going up at a time when spending is coming down," said John Dickinson, a stores "watcher" with Chase Manhattan Securities.

Retailers who stand to lose are those like Dixons, Currys, Storehouse (BHS, Mothercare and Habitat), Next and, to a lesser extent, Woolworth and Boots. They specialise in luxury items that have been snapped up as fast as people have got their tax cuts.

But the one thing that may actually maintain spending is the use of store charge cards and credit cards. These have been less sensitive to changes in base rates. People prepared to pay an annual rate on a charge card of anything between 23 and 30 per cent, or even more, are unlikely to blink at interest rates of 12 per cent.

Although people are now becoming aware of the amount of interest they are paying, it is unlikely to put a block on the use of plastic. It is even less noticeable since interest on credit cards is paid monthly and people have got used to splashing out £10 every four weeks for their £500 loan.

So with less cash in their pockets, shoppers may resort to plastic and paying on the "never, never" which will eventually feed into the economy and start the whole merry-go-round off again. That is, of course, if higher mortgage payments do not quash our thirst for spending totally.

Credit cards are an area of spending which have so far avoided the Chancellor's "belt-tightening" scrutiny since, if mortgages are excluded, credit cards still only make up 10 per cent of Britain's total personal borrowing.

If American Express and Diners Club are excluded, turn-over in bank credit cards last year amounted to £17 billion while store cards — a small but growing part of the retailers' business as they expand into financial services — took £4 billion.

So the question is: will the Chancellor's policy work? One problem is that the impact of the interest rate tightening takes time to work through the system. Many building societies do not like the hassle and expense of writing to borrowers, telling them their new repayment rates, and stick to doing it once a year.

Although you get charged from the date of the increase, it may be months before you start paying. As many as 40 per cent of building society borrowers come under this kind of annual review system. So it will be a while before the Chancellor knows if his "touch on the brakes" has been hard enough and the lag will be compounded as people take time to readjust to their new spending power.

There is also another side to the interest rate equation. Just as home loan rates are going up, so are savings' rates. So for the cash being soaked up in higher payments on home loans, there is a matching flow of extra interest to depositors. That in turn is available, though not necessarily used, for extra spending.

One factor which might offset this is that depositors may not regard an extra few points on the interest rates as the trigger for additional spending. And as the BSA said in its July bulletin, higher mortgage rates could affect the demand for mortgages, new houses and consumer goods.

But although the BSA says it is difficult to draw firm conclusions about the economic impact of mortgage rate changes, it suggests that "if one of the reasons for increasing the general level of interest rates is to reduce the post mortgage payment disposable income of borrowers, then interest rate policy has become a blunter tool".

It will be some months before the economic impact of that policy becomes clear. We have already started paying.

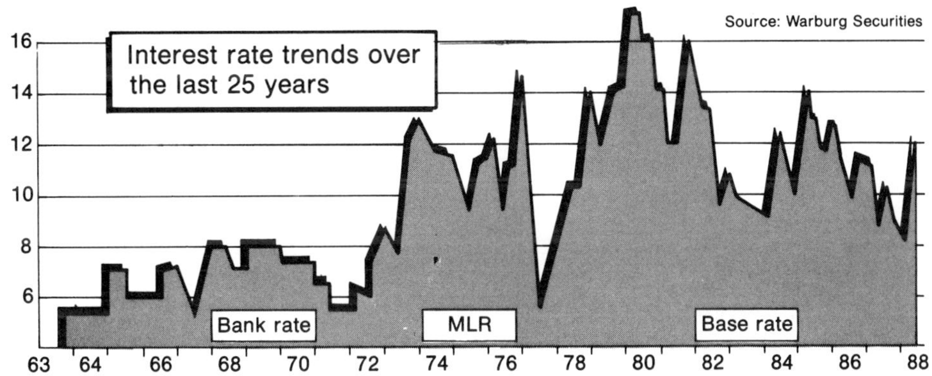

SOURCE: THE GUARDIAN, 27 AUGUST 1988

a Visit a local bank and find out what the 'base rate' is at present.

b Why are credit card holders willing to carry on borrowing as interest rates rise?

c i) Why might the Chancellor of the Exchequer wish to reduce demand in the economy?
ii) What are the dangers in relying solely on interest rates to try to control demand?

d Why might high interest rates
i) benefit banks and building societies
ii) harm manufacturers and exporters?

e Apart from the groups mentioned in (d), who benefits and who loses when interest rates rise while income tax rates fall?

UNEMPLOYMENT ·1·

EXERCISE 63

Study this graph.

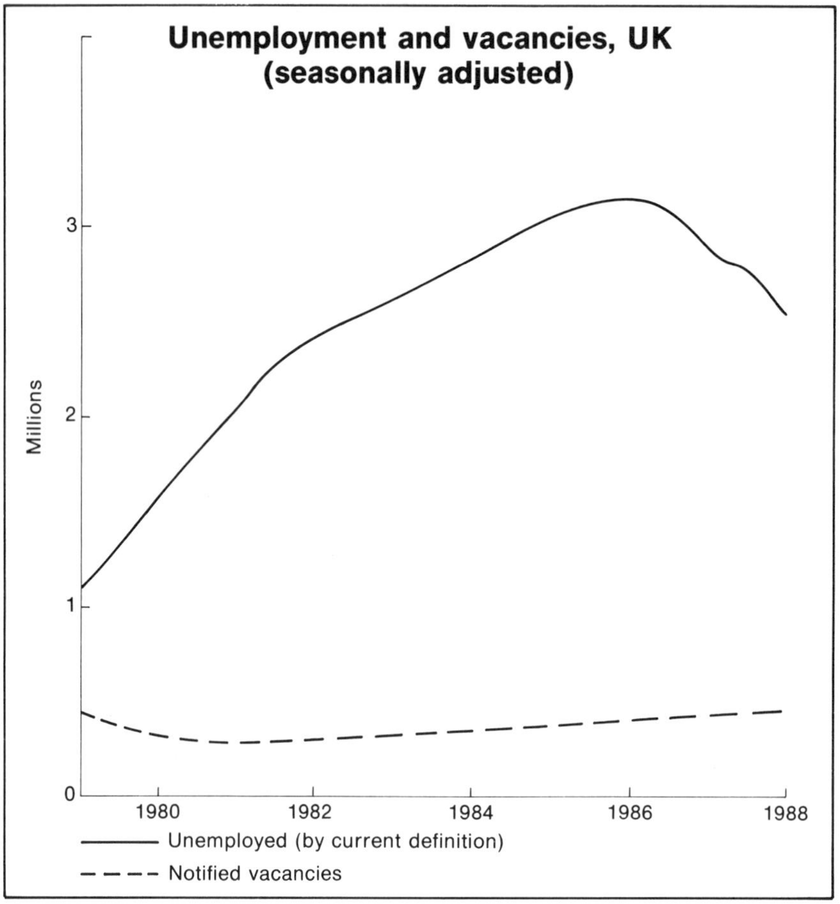

SOURCE: ECONOMIC TRENDS, 1988

a Explain why the phrase 'seasonally adjusted' is important when considering unemployment figures.

b The government has made a large number of changes to the way in which unemployment figures are calculated. People seeking work are now only included in the unemployment figures if they are claiming state benefit. Without these changes, many economists claim that unemployment would have reached more than 3.5 million in 1986. From the graph, estimate how many people have been removed from the official figures by these changes.

c In October 1987 the unemployment rate fell to below 10 per cent of the total labour force for the first time in five years. Suggest reasons for this.

d Why are there always jobs available as 'notified vacancies' even though people are unemployed?

UNEMPLOYMENT ·2·

EXERCISE 64

Study this information.

Unemployment rates adjusted to OECD concepts: international comparison

Percentages

	Annual averages											
	1970	1976	1977	1978	1979	1980	1981	1982	1983	1984	1985	1986
United Kingdom	3.0	5.6	6.1	5.9	5.0	6.4	9.8	11.3	12.5	11.7	11.2	11.1
Belgium	2.1	6.4	7.4	7.9	8.2	8.8	10.8	12.6	12.1	12.1	11.2	10.8
France	2.4	4.4	4.9	5.2	5.9	6.3	7.4	8.1	8.3	9.7	10.1	10.3
Italy	5.3	6.6	7.0	7.1	7.6	7.5	8.3	9.0	9.8	10.2	10.5	—
Netherlands	1.0	5.5	5.3	5.3	5.4	6.0	8.5	11.4	12.0	11.8	10.6	9.9
Spain	2.4	4.6	5.2	6.9	8.5	11.2	13.9	15.8	17.2	20.0	21.4	21.0
Australia	1.6	4.7	5.6	6.2	6.2	6.0	5.7	7.1	9.9	8.9	8.2	8.0
Canada	5.6	7.1	8.0	8.3	7.4	7.4	7.5	10.9	11.8	11.2	10.4	9.5
Japan	1.1	2.0	2.0	2.2	2.1	2.0	2.2	2.4	2.6	2.7	2.6	2.8
Sweden	1.5	1.6	1.8	2.2	2.1	2.0	2.5	3.2	3.5	3.1	2.8	2.7
United States	4.8	7.6	6.9	6.0	5.8	7.0	7.5	9.5	9.5	7.4	7.1	6.9

The Organisation for Economic Co-operation and Development (OECD) standardised rates for unemployment in selected countries are shown.

These rates are estimated by OECD to conform, as far as possible, to International Labour Organisation guidelines, and they are calculated as percentages of the total labour force. The term 'unemployed' covers all people who are without work, are available for work and are seeking employment for pay or profit. Between 1980 and 1982 the average unemployment rate rose in all the countries shown and in 1982 it was above 10 per cent in the United Kingdom, Spain, Belgium, Canada and the Netherlands. The unemployment rate also reached 10 per cent in Italy in 1984 and in France in 1985.

SOURCE: SOCIAL TRENDS, 1988

a Which country shown on the chart has had the greatest increase in unemployment rates since 1970?

b Within many of the countries shown on the chart there is a problem of regional unemployment. Name some areas of the UK where unemployment is likely to be well above and below the national average, and give reasons.

c The unemployment rate has increased in all the countries listed over the period shown in the chart. Suggest reasons for this.

d Some economists have stated that the problem of world-wide unemployment is a 'time bomb'. Do you agree?

STANDARDS OF LIVING

EXERCISE 65

This chart shows how long someone on the average hourly wage rate has to work so that his or her net income pays for various items.

Time to pay

Item	Year			
	1971		1986	
	Hours	Minutes	Hours	Minutes
	00	09	00	07
	00	05	00	04
	00	13	00	12
	00	55	01	15
	01	04	01	03
	00	33	00	26
	39	59	25	38
	00	22	00	22
	01	19	01	26
	03	16	01	37

SOURCE: SOCIAL TRENDS, 1988

a How are the times shown in the chart affected by
- i) prices
- ii) wage rates
- iii) taxes?

b Would you say that the length of working time needed to pay for a colour television set has increased or decreased since colour television was introduced in Britain? Give reasons for your answer.

c With reference to the chart, explain why it would be more difficult to calculate the time needed to pay for an 'average weekly gas bill' than a 'pint of beer'.

d Compare the length of time needed to pay a gas bill in 1971 and 1986 with the time needed to pay an electricity bill. Give possible reasons for the changes indicated by these figures.

e Find out how much you would earn per hour if you took a part-time job at a local supermarket. Find out the prices of the following items, and calculate the length of time (in hours and minutes) you would have to work to pay for them:
- i) fish and chips for two people
- ii) a compact disc
- iii) a pair of good quality school shoes
- iv) a colour TV licence
- v) a three-piece suite
- vi) a two-week holiday in Mallorca in August for a family of four
- vii) a medium sized family car

f Would you expect the length of time needed to work to cover the monthly mortgage repayment for an average semi-detached house to increase or decrease over the next ten years? Give reasons for your answer.

THE COST OF LIVING

EXERCISE 66

Examine the chart, which shows how some of the statistics concerning the purchase of an average semi-detached house have changed over the years.

HOW SEMI PRICES HAVE RISEN SINCE 1930

	House price	Average wkly wage	Interest and mthly cost	Home own'shp
1930	£500	£4	5%, £2.70	20%
1960	£2,690	£14	6%, £14	43%
1970	£5,280	£24	8½%, £32	51%
1986	£40,000	£185	11%, £285	62%

SOURCE: DAILY MIRROR, 19 OCTOBER 1986

a Calculate how the ratio of house prices to annual incomes has changed since 1930.

b Why has home ownership increased at the same time as house prices and interest rates?

c i) Explain what is meant by the 'mobility of labour'.
ii) How is the mobility of labour affected by the fact that house prices in the South East are much higher than in other parts of the country?
iii) Why is the mobility of labour important to British industry?

d Name some businesses which benefit from high house prices, and others which suffer. Explain your answers.

e During December 1988 the Chancellor of the Exchequer suggested that mortgage repayments should NOT be included in the Retail Price Index, which measures the rate of inflation (or cost of living). Do you agree?

GOVERNMENT REVENUE

EXERCISE 67

Examine this diagram, which represents the percentages of different types of government revenue.

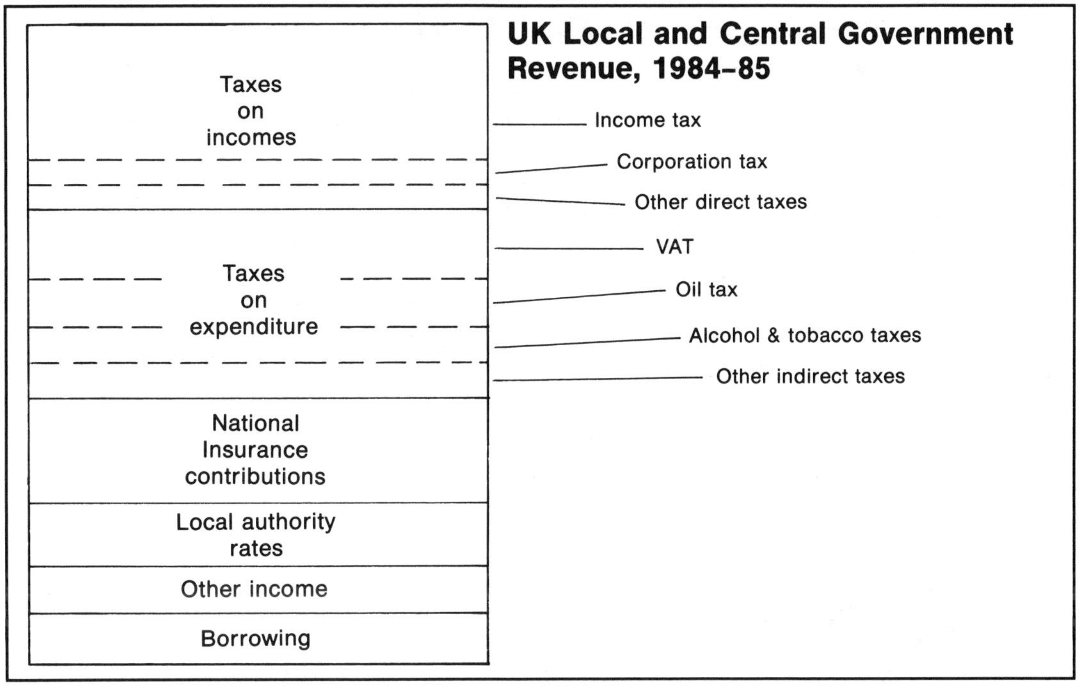

SOURCE: ECONOMIC PROGRESS REPORT, MARCH 1984

a Most people pay income tax through the PAYE system. What do these initials stand for?

b Who pays corporation tax?

c What do the initials VAT stand for?

d Explain the difference between 'direct' and 'indirect' taxation.

e Local Authority Rates are due to be replaced by a poll tax called the *Community Charge*.
i) Explain what is meant by the term 'poll tax'.
ii) Why do many people regard poll taxes as being unfair?

f Describe the main taxes paid by
i) a sole trader running a corner shop
ii) a public limited company operating a large factory

g In 1988 the Chancellor of the Exchequer had a 'Balanced Budget'. What does this mean, and which item would it affect on the diagram?

PUBLIC SPENDING

EXERCISE 68

Study this diagram, which illustrates UK government expenditure.

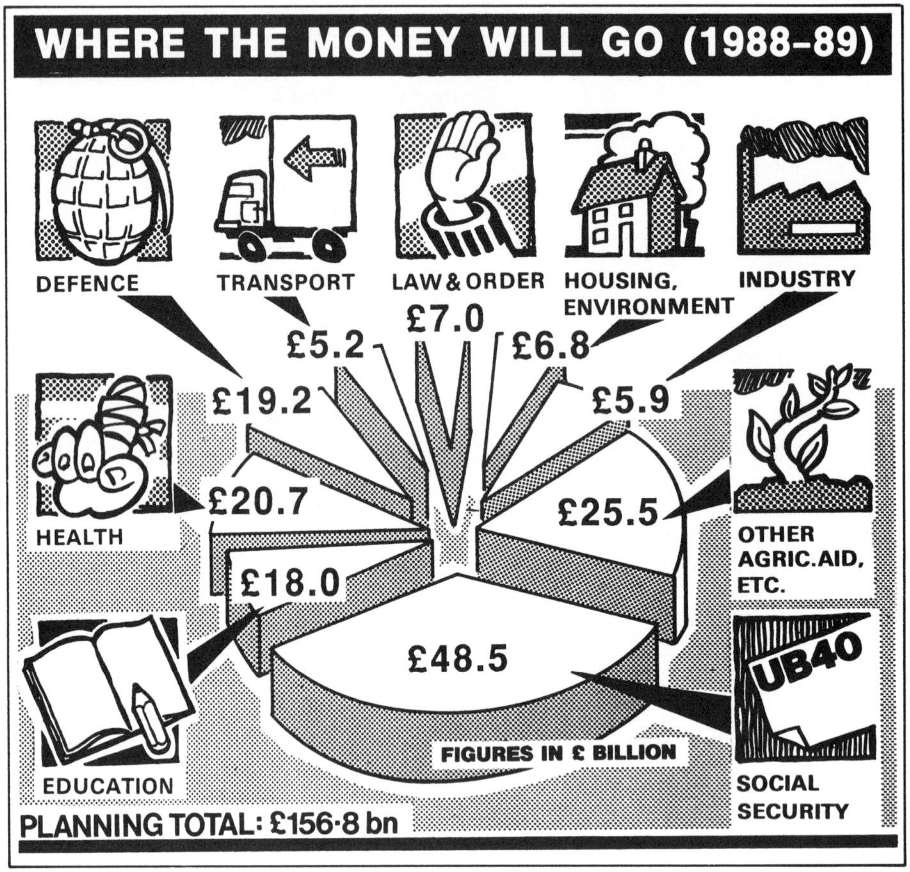

SOURCE: THE GUARDIAN, 4 NOVEMBER 1987

a What is the largest category of expenditure illustrated here? Give reasons why this category has grown over the last ten years.

b What is the second largest category of expenditure illustrated here? Why might Britain's membership of the EEC help to explain why this category is so large?

c In what ways does the government spend money on Industry?

d Why might this category get smaller in future years?

e In what ways does the government spend money on Transport?

f Explain why this category of expenditure is important to business.

g Government expenditure can be classified as either 'capital' or 'current'. Explain the difference, and give examples of each from the category of Education.

h Each year the Government produces a list of its priorities in spending, together with its plans for raising the necessary money. Which Government Minister is responsible for announcing this 'list', and what is the announcement called?

i Why are politicians interested in the relative sizes of categories such as Health, Education and Defence?

j Explain how Health differs from Social Security.

k Health and Social Security were under the overall control of a single cabinet minister until August 1988 when the Prime Minister split them into two separate ministries. What arguments can be put forward in support of this change?

EXCISE DUTIES

EXERCISE 69

Study the following diagram carefully.

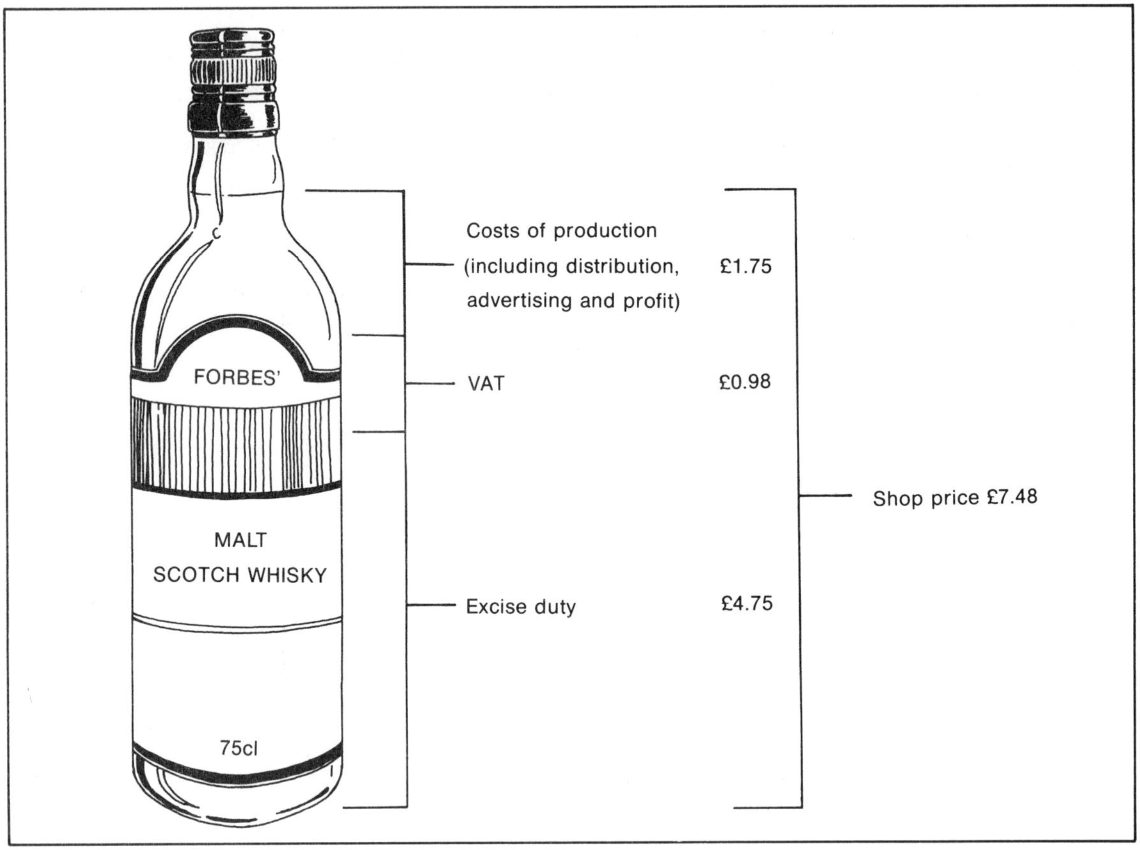

SOURCE: ECONOMIC TRENDS, 1988

a What is an excise duty?

b i) What is the current rate of VAT?
ii) Who determines the rate of VAT?

c Why would an increase in alcohol duties be supported by the anti-alcohol pressure groups?

d What is the main problem with increasing indirect taxes?

e i) Explain in your own words how the costs of a typical bottle of wine are broken down.
ii) How might the shop prices of items such as wine, sherry and whisky be affected by the single European market in 1992?

f Why are petrol, alcohol, tobacco and gambling more heavily taxed than other items?

THE ROAD LOBBY

Study this newspaper article.

Inadequate roads will stifle Britain's economic growth

Unless more funds are made available for road improvements the country's economic growth will be stifled, warns Mr Jeffrey Rose, Chairman of the RAC.

The RAC is urging the Chancellor of the Exchequer to give much greater priority to road requirements when assessing the merits of competing bids by Government Departments for public expenditure.

Mr Rose points out: "Much public expenditure is absorbed by services and projects which, however desirable individually, constitute straightforward consumption of resources. The provision of an adequate road system is not consumption of wealth — it is an essential investment in and for our future economic prosperity. An efficient road infrastructure is as essential to industry and commerce as modern factories, offices and telecommunications.

"There is now some recognition of this by the Department of Transport but in the absence of adequate central funding the Department is driven to speculate about the possibility of private financing in circumstances which have not been defined and with the implication of tolls to be imposed on drivers to service this private capital."

Mr Rose adds: "This approach is neither desirable nor necessary. Taxation of road users in the current financial year will amount to about £16,000 million. As against this under £4,000 million will be spent on roads for construction, maintenance and support services such as police."

In its submission to the Chancellor, the RAC states: "Whatever may be the merits of proposals to incur public expenditure for various other necessary or desirable purposes, there is much demonstrable and increasing evidence that expansion and improvement of the main road network — as well as an enlarged programme to complete unavoidable maintenance work — must be achieved extremely rapidly and needs to be given priority." Mr Rose stresses the national dependence on road transport which accounts for 90 per cent of all movements of freight and people.

"The total of vehicles licensed is growing by over 2 per cent annually. Total mileage travelled is growing by a significantly higher figure. Even the most conservative calculations suggest that the increase in traffic by say the year 2000 will be at least 30 per cent.

"Already there are daily reports by the media of serious hold-ups causing chaos in the main road network in almost all parts of the country. The total cost of this congestion is immense."

The RAC's submission warns the Chancellor: "If the Government fails to initiate rapid action to retrieve the situation now, future generations will inherit a chaotic road transport system and the economic growth the nation would otherwise have enjoyed will be greatly diminished."

SOURCE: BRIDGEND RECORDER, 5 JANUARY 1989 (BASED ON AN RAC PRESS RELEASE)

a The so-called 'road lobby' consists of several 'interest groups' which represent individuals and organisations wishing the Government to spend more money on roads. The RAC claims to represent motorists; what other interest groups might wish to see an increase in road construction?

b Write a press release on behalf of the 'rail lobby', stating why the Government should invest more money in Britain's railways.

PRESSURE GROUPS

EXERCISE 71

Read this newspaper article.

Greenpeace in polar stand-off

Paul Brown, aboard the Gondwana, in Antarctica

LEADERS of a Greenpeace expedition to Antarctica were squaring up for a clash today with French construction workers who they say are going to blast away penguin breeding colonies to build an airstrip.

After a two-hour meeting yesterday at the Dumont d'Urville research base, Mr Peter Wilkinson, the Greenpeace group's leader, warned the French that they would take direct action to halt the project.

The 30-strong crew of the Greenpeace ship Gondwana face a specially imported French production team of 33, equipped with heavy moving equipment and explosives and anxious to get on with the job in the two months left before work becomes impossible because of the weather. In addition, the French base has a staff of 150.

The French say they need the airstrip to improve access to research facilities. But Greenpeace officials fear it will be the first step in a rush to exploit the Antarctic's minerals. The explosives being used, they add, are destroying the breeding grounds of 75,000 Adélie penguins on the rocky islands.

The French deny any attempt to pre-empt ratification of the newly signed international minerals convention. Mr Michel Engler, the project's manager, said a consortium of French companies had shown interest, but only to test their products in a cold climate.

He announced that the French Government had plans to build a much larger scientific base 1,000 kilometres inland using the new airstrip as a supply base.

Mr Paul Bogart from Greenpeace argued that building the new base could not justify destruction of the penguin colonies. The French, he said, were breaking the Antarctic Treaty by destroying wildlife. Ironically, the research station was originally set up to study penguins.

Two hours of talks broke up with Mr Wilkinson telling Mr Jean-Francis Houssin, chief executive of the French territorial claim, that his crew would mount demonstrations to halt the work.

The Gondwana, which sailed from Auckland on December 22, arrived at the base on Thursday. It anchored about half a mile from where the French intend to blow the tops off six rocky islands and push the debris into the sea to make a causeway between them.

Mr Engler told the Greenpeace team that the French regretted the destruction of the penguins' habitat. In order to minimise the problem, they were taking fertile eggs from breeding birds in the path of the airstrip and replacing them with plastic ones. The fertile eggs were being taken to another colony in the hope that penguins there would be able to raise additional chicks.

A nearby Emperor penguin colony which uses the islands to reach its feeding ground would be helped by the construction programme, he added, because they would find it easier to get over the levelled ground.

As far as he knew, there was no oil in the immediate area, nor had commercially exploitable minerals been found in the French-claimed territory.

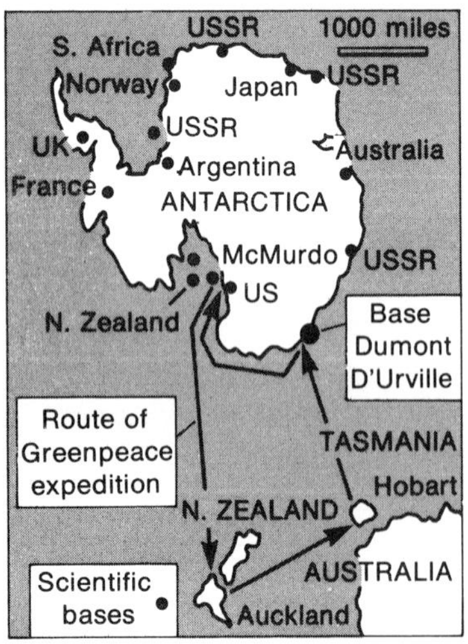

SOURCE: THE GUARDIAN, 7 JANUARY 1989
MAP © PAUL BROWN

a Why might multi-national companies be interested in Antarctica?

b Why is Greenpeace concerned about this interest?

c Greenpeace is a 'pressure group'. Explain what this term means.

d Friends of the Earth is another environmental pressure group. Among the issues it has tackled recently are acid rain, the ozone layer, the 'greenhouse' effect and the destruction of rain forests. Follow the news for a few weeks and make a note of any references to these issues.

e Why should these issues be regarded as important by
- i) individuals
- ii) governments
- iii) businesses?

POLLUTION

Read this newspaper article.

Pollution in River Taff

Echo Reporter

WELSH WATER officials investigating a major pollution incident in the River Taff were due to hold talks with the chiefs of a Merthyr factory today.

The pollution affected a five-mile stretch of the river from Abercanaid to Quakers Yard during the weekend, and killed around 7,000 trout, 400 roach, and other smaller fish.

Local anglers, who have worked for several years to stock the river with fish described themselves as "badly hit" by the pollution.

After two days of tests by scientists trying to find the source of the pollution, Welsh Water identified the substance as an industrial acid.

Affected

Welsh Water spokesman Mr Rod MacKay says: "Our staff will be talking with some of the people who were involved in operations at a factory in the area during the weekend."

"Our scientists will also be preparing a report on the extent to which the smaller life-forms in the river have been affected," he said.

Mr MacKay added the pollution killed nearly all the fish in the river as far as Quakers Yard, where the Taf Bargoed joins the main river and diluted the pollution.

People in the Merthyr area have been warned not to eat any of the dead fish in case they are contaminated with a substance which is also harmful to humans.

"It will take some time for the river to recover to the same standard of fishing. It is a bit early to say how long it will take," Mr MacKay says.

SOURCE: SOUTH WALES ECHO, 26 OCTOBER 1988

a Explain carefully the meaning of the terms:
 i) private costs
 ii) external costs
 iii) social costs

b Give four examples of private costs which might have to be paid by the factory mentioned in the article.

c Explain how this firm has created an external cost.

d Besides the firm itself, name three groups of people who might have to pay for the social costs of this pollution.

e Suppose you lived in a community which is affected by industrial pollution. Outline the steps that could be taken to try to improve matters.

TEACHER'S NOTES
Selected answers and comments

1 With a bit of prompting, students should come to realise that the network of processes and raw materials involved in making an apparently simple object like a pencil (e.g. discovering how graphite is manufactured, tracing the wood back to Norway, the rubber back to Malaysia, etc.), are no less interesting than those of a more sophisticated item such as a Midi hi-fi.

2 **(b)** iv) The historical trend would reflect the drift of working population away from the land. As national income rises, in most countries, a decreasing proportion of income is spent on food (to economists this is known as *Engel's Law*) and increasing proportions are spent on manufactured goods and services. Thus the agricultural sector contracts, while the manufacturing and service sectors expand. In developed countries the tertiary sector usually becomes the largest of the three.

4 **(a)** ii) Recovered coal is obtained from sources such as old coal tips. In the past, the methods used to separate coal from waste products were inefficient, and left quantities of useful coal on the waste tips which can be economically recovered today.

6 **(c)** Some economists have argued that Britain's record deficits during 1988 were a *good* sign, as they indicated that Britain was importing raw materials in order to manufacture exports. However, there was no sign of the upturn in exports which would bear this out.

7 **(e)** The chart shows *percentages*, not absolute amounts. Therefore the size of the imports block is equal to that of the exports block, both signifying 100 per cent.

9 **(b)** ii) The Government has spent millions of pounds in advertising the share issues; it also helped to underwrite the flotation of BP during the Stock Market crash of 1987. These costs must be subtracted from the gross figures to arrive at the net figures.

10 **(a)** A public utility is generally understood to be a business organisation providing a public amenity (e.g. supplying water, gas or electricity) and subject to special governmental regulation because of the importance of the amenity to the public. Students might like to debate whether *telephones* should be regarded as a utility.
(b) Utilities tend to be *natural monopolies*, which means that they are services which are provided at lower cost by a single producer rather than by several (this is because of the massive capital infrastructure required, and the wasteful duplication of resources which would exist with more than one supplier). If unregulated, the abuse of monopoly power could bring massive profits to privatised utilities.
(e) Many individual shareholders would appear to have invested for short-term profit; shares become concentrated in the hands of institutional investors, which take a longer-term view.

15 **(c)** Approximately 5 tons of raw materials make 1 ton of steel. A pint of beer is over 90 per cent water.
(d) Transport costs make it economic to manufacture steel as near as possible to its source of raw materials (in modern terms, a deep-water port where iron-ore can be imported), while it makes sense to allow the water mains to transport water to the breweries, which are located as close as possible to the population centres.

(g) Since the establishment of a National Grid, firms using electrically powered machines have not been tied to power sources. Modern electronic technology has accelerated this trend. Footloose firms are more interested in such things as: the nature of the site (they often insist on 'greenfield' sites), the availability of government grants, the quality of local housing and other infrastructure, access to markets (particularly the EEC), etc.

16 **(b)** i) Average earnings; migration rates; ownership of houses, cars, etc.; age structure of the population; take-up of social welfare payments; hospital waiting lists; mortality rates; participation rates (proportion of men to women in employment); etc.

17 **(e)** As suggested in (b), the figures in Table 2 correlate less well than those in other tables.
(f) These include high-tech firms with aggressive marketing (Amstrad), and rapidly-expanding firms in the service sector (Kuoni). They haven't yet suffered diseconomies of scale.
(h) It depends what you mean by Shell! Table 1 refers to the UK subsidiary, Table 8 to the multinational conglomerate.
(i) High costs.

18 **(f)** Brand names are increasingly recognised as an 'intangible' but nevertheless valuable asset. Accountants now include an estimated value of a company's brand names in company balance sheets. This practice is controversial. Students could be asked for ideas on how they would go about putting a monetary value on a brand name such as *Fry's Turkish Delight*.

19 **(d)** There has been some press criticism of the 'cereal bar' market for purveying a healthy, wholesome image which, it is alleged, might not be entirely justified in every case.

25 **(a)** Mastercard = Access (Lloyds, Midland, National Westminster)
Visa = Chase Manhattan, Robert Fleming, TSB, Barclaycard, Building Society Credit Cards.
Chase Manhattan and Robert Fleming compete with each other in offering the lowest APR available: both offer rates substantially below those of other credit cards. Students could be asked to consider why people appear to be willing to pay such high interest rates.

26 At the time of writing the Government was considering an offer for the purchase of National Girobank from the Alliance and Leicester Building Society.

27 Students can answer these questions verbally, or with the use of supply and demand curves.

28 The disc jockey Paul Gambaccini has stated (Radio 4 interview, 3.2.89) that the record companies themselves are killing the singles market, by re-releasing single hits on 'compilation albums'. He believes that record companies are failing to recognise that there is a continuing potential market for singles, as people like to listen to tunes which come and go with a relatively short time span.

One aspect of the marketing of singles which students might find interesting to consider is the quality of the B side. There have been occasions when the B side has become equally popular to, or even more popular than the A side (at least one of the authors can remember *Juliet* by the Four Pennies and *Penny Lane* by the Beatles), but usually the B side is an inferior offering.

In February 1989 one of the smaller recording companies announced that it will begin issuing single-sided discs which will sell at 99p. This significant price advantage over double-sided singles might revitalise the market if other companies follow suit.

There is also the possibility of the CD single. A bank of CD singles placed in a CD player with 'random play' facility would give a total playing time comparable to that of one side of a conventional LP record.

31 **(f)** These brand names have entered the English language as generic terms for all similar products. Thus we speak of *hoovering* the carpet, whether the vacuum cleaner is a Hoover or not. Students might come up with ideas why this has not always happened (cars are not universally known as *Fords*, nor radios as *Marconies*. They might also come up with suggestions for further brand names to add to the list: possibilities include *Superglue* and *Cornflakes*.

33 **(b)** Expect reference to cost structure of firm; mark-up.
(e) The UK primary industry is oil.

35 **(b)** The main assets of a bank are cash, loans, investments, stocks and shares.
(e) The main liabilities are its customers' accounts, i.e. deposit and current accounts.

37 **(d)** Though fewer retail outlets in 1984, turnover has increased because:
i) size of retail outlets increased,
ii) consumer spending increased.

39 **(a)** Students will need to refer to the graph.

40 **(b)** Space refers to distance and transport. Time refers to storage facilities.

41 **(a)** Divide answer into: i) external economies, e.g. banking and finance services; ii) internal economies, e.g. management and production economies.

42 **(b)** i) Freightliner.

44 **(a)** Possible reasons: larger population, fewer cars produced, lower incomes, so fewer people able to afford cars which can be regarded as luxury items, perhaps fewer people able to drive due to lack of opportunity.
(e) No, not necessarily. We would also need to know population figures before answering this.

46 **(b)** It would be better for each group to hold its own meeting at this stage, rather than have a whole-class meeting, if the classroom is large enough to accommodate several meetings taking place at once. The teacher could have a quiet word with 'Tracy' so that she can decide whether she really did it or not.

49 The second graph is not easy to follow and requires some considerable care in interpretation. It shows, for example, that no workers covered by the agreements mentioned had basic entitlements to five or more weeks holiday until approx. 1980, and that in 1986 no workers covered by these agreements had less than 4 weeks entitlement. In 1961 approx. 95 per cent had 2 weeks entitlement; in 1986 approx. 15 per cent had 4 weeks, approx. another 60 per cent had 4–5 weeks, and the rest had five or more weeks. The main point to get across to students is that on the second graph, a downward sloping line indicates an increased entitlement to holidays.

51 **(b)** The main problem of measuring the effects of industrial disputes is *what* to measure? Possibilities are: lost production, working hours, lost profits, number of disputes, etc.
(c) i) Growth of service sectors and general decline of UK manufacturing industry.
ii) Manufacturing becoming more capital-intensive.
iii) Government policy — trades union legislation.
iv) Private working agreements — the Japanese experience.

52 **(a)** Answer should be divided into: i) letter services, ii) parcel services.

54 **(a)** *Picture 1.* Consumer Protection Department should be informed. Sale of Goods Act and Food and Drugs Act.
Picture 2. Health and Safety at Work Act. For unfair dismissal see union representative and could consider industrial tribunal.
Picture 3. No rights to demand a refund, there has been no breach of contract. However, some shops will allow exchange.
Picture 4. Exclusion clauses are not binding if a court finds they are 'unreasonable'. Contact Consumer Protection, or Citizens' Advice Bureau.
Picture 5. Legal tender: 50p and 20p coins up to £10
10p and 5p coins up to £5
2p and 1p coins up to 20p
Picture 6. H.P. agreements have 'cooling off' period — 5 days from receiving second copy of agreement. More rights if agreement signed in your own home.

56 **(c)** The obvious ones: fire, flood, theft.
The less obvious ones: business interruption, fidelity guarantee, employers' liability.

60 **(c)** Mail order through advertising. Catalogues: Kays, Freemans, etc.
'Direct mail': publications such as *Readers' Digest*.

61 **(b)** iii) A typical business plan: ideas, resources and abilities.

62 **(c)** i) If rate of interest rises it encourages savings, but it discourages investment. This will mean less finance available to UK industries, which could lead to a fall in output and thus employment. Also there will be an effect on the balance of payments and the exchange rate. Capital funds will flow into the country, the exchange rate rises so exports become less competitive and imports more attractive.

63 **(a)** 'Seasonally adjusted' allows for peaks and troughs at certain times of the year, e.g. school leavers in September.
(d) Frictional unemployment (short-term unemployment which arises because people who leave one job do not immediately take up their next post).

64 **(d)** 'Time bomb' refers to a situation in the long run which will lead to severe pressures of poverty, low standards of housing, roads, hospitals and schools. Also an unfair distribution of income and wealth which could lead to a 'divided' society and discontentment.

65 **(a)** i) prices rise, time rises
ii) wages rise, time falls
iii) taxes rise, time rises

(b) Time falls because colour television relatively cheaper.
(c) Gas bills affected by climate and so vary from quarter to quarter. Also, insulation can affect gas bills.
(f) Depends on type of mortgage and interest rates.

66 (b) i) preferences of owning your own home
ii) government incentives, i.e. tax relief on mortgages
iii) government policies to sell off council houses
iv) higher rents
v) higher incomes — as incomes rise faster than prices
vi) mortgages more easily available

67 (g) Borrowing would disappear. Taxes on income might be affected.

68 (k) The main arguments: both are large departments, social security growing at a fast rate as unemployment rises. Also they cover completely separate areas.

70 (a) Interest groups: CBI for industry, especially the car and civil engineering industry. Road Hauliers Association. Residents near busy traffic to relieve road congestion.

72 (b) i) compensation to Water Authority for dead fish
ii) fine for polluting the river
iii) compensation to Water Authority for expenses incurred in using scientists
iv) cost to the firm of installing equipment to ensure this will not happen again

TOPIC INDEX (The numbers referred to are exercise numbers)